WORKING MY "BUT" OFF!

Reflections of a Property Investor

Dave Ives

Copyright © 2014 by Dave Ives

All rights reserved.

ISBN-13: 978-1511939577
ISBN-10: 1511939575

CONTENTS

1. But, what do you mean by, "Working my BUT off?" 1
2. But, who is this guy? 3
3. But, why write this book? 7
4. But, how do I get motivated to become financially independent? 17
5. But, what if I've got a good job? 41
6. But, what if I fail? 58
7. But, how do I get started? 79
8. But, what if I can't even get a loan for a mobile home? 97
9. But, how do I get my first rental property? 120
10. But, how do I know if it's a good buy? 134
11. But, how do I negotiate? 151
12. But, what if I'm no good at maintenance and repairs? 159
13. But, what if I lose my job? 169
14. But, where do I go from here? 193

Recommended Reading List 201
About the Author 203

1 BUT, WHAT DO YOU MEAN BY, "WORKING MY BUT OFF?"

Before achieving financial independence through property investing, I had to work my BUT off! It seemed like every time I wanted to move forward a BUT question would appear.

> *But, what if it doesn't work?*
>
> *But, what if people laugh at me?*
>
> *But, what if it's the wrong decision?*

And the list of BUT questions went on and on and on.

The biggest problem with BUT questions is they tend to be negative. They tend to hold me back. They tend to stop me in my tracks. So, I had only one choice - I had to work them off! Work my BUT off!

Dave Ives

Guess what?

I'm still working them off! I still have challenges with my – always popping up at the wrong time – BUT questions!

That's OK. It's part of life. I just have to remember to keep working my BUT off – it never stops.

2 BUT, WHO IS THIS GUY?

Hello! I'm Dave Ives. Glad you're here. I put this book together to share my story. The story of how I worked off a bunch of BUT questions to achieve my goal of financial independence. I just kept working my BUT off until I made it!

It took a long time. A few weeks after my 49th birthday, I delivered a short but important speech. I delivered it to my boss, only two words – "I quit!"

Boy it felt good to say that!

I haven't had a job – or a pay check – since.

So, how do I live without a job? How do I live without a pay check? What do I do for money?

Well, it turns out, long before I quit my job, I planted a lot of "money seeds." I made sure there was some money left over each month and planted it in residential rental properties. After repeating this process over many years, the "crop" finally came up

– harvest time. The seeds grew into mighty trees and started producing fruit – lots of fruit!

So, even though I no longer have a job, I still have income. Virtually all of my income today comes from residential investment property.

When I first started planting my property investment crop, the harvest was pretty thin. OK, it was pretty near zero. OK, it was negative a lot of the time! I remember some months – especially when big maintenance bills came in – when I had to pay for the privilege of planting. I had to pay to keep the farm going. I had to pay to stay in the property investing business! In other words, I was losing money.

Not exciting.

But, just like the farmer, I knew I had to plant. I had to put seeds in the ground. And, just like the farmer, I knew the crop could fail. All my work could be for nothing.

So, why bother?

Well, it's very simple. It's very basic. If you plant, there's a possibility of a harvest. If you don't plant ... forget it! There's a 100% guarantee ... NO HARVEST!

I knew I had to plant. I knew it involved risk. I knew it involved making a few financial sacrifices - nothing too extreme. Maybe living in a more modest home; maybe driving a second hand car; maybe holding off on buying the latest gadgets. No big deal.

WORKING MY "BUT" OFF!

I'm not a big time, high rolling – master negotiating – property investor. I'm just a guy who made the transition from the just-over-broke (JOB) world into the world of financial independence via property investing.

For big-time property investment advice, I'd recommend reading Donald Trump or Robert Kiyosaki.

Why would I write a property investing book when you can read the wisdom of these guys and many others who are masters in the game? I've benefited from their wisdom – I've read a lot of their books. I still read and re-read them!

So, who am I to write another property investment book?

Why would I do it?

I wouldn't (at least not yet!) and I didn't.

This book is about building belief. When you're done reading it I would love to hear you say something like, "If this guy can reach financial independence, I know I can!"

That's the goal. That's the aim.

I want to share with you a few of the obstacles I overcame in my journey. I want to share some of the insights I picked up along the way. I want to let you know you can achieve financial independence and exit the JOB world too. Let you know, there is a way out.

The way out begins with you believing it's possible. And, that's where I come in. I'm here to help you get that belief.

Once you've got the belief, nothing will stop you. Doors will open, the right teachers will appear, you'll absorb the information, you'll take action – you'll be on your way!

If I can play a positive role toward helping you achieve your life goals and dreams, then I'll be happy – very happy, for both you and me!

Well, this is supposed to be the chapter where I establish my credibility - what makes me qualified to write this book. I thought about putting in my resume or writing a little biography but on further reflection I realized – forget it, way too corporate, way too boring!

So, if I've failed to establish credibility in this opening salvo, hopefully I'll correct the deficiency as you read my stories about how I worked my BUT off to achieve my goal – financial independence!

Wishing you Godspeed on your life journey!

3 BUT, WHY WRITE THIS BOOK?

Why write this book?

Why not?

I've been a full time property investor since July 2009. I made the transition from the JOB (just-over-broke) world to financial independence. I figured there may be some people out there who might be interested in making the same transition.

Why not share some of my thoughts and insights? Why not share some of my experiences? Why not give others belief so they make the transition too?

Why property investing?

Was my goal to become a full time property investor?

No.

My goal was very simple. I wanted to become financially independent.

What does that mean?

Well, for me it means I'm not financially dependent on any of the following:

> *A job*
> *A boss*
> *A pay check*
> *A company*
> *A government*

It means creating my own wealth based on income producing capital growth assets. In my case these assets happen to be residential homes.

Because I achieved financial independence through property investing, I call myself a property investor. Property investing is the vehicle I used to achieve my goal.

Not easy!

My journey to financial independence took a lot of turns, detours, side-tracks and setbacks. It hasn't been easy.

I had a late start. Yes, I bought my first investment property – a residential block of land in Florida – at age 23, but I didn't own an income generating rental property until age 33. I'd call that a late start.

WORKING MY "BUT" OFF!

Initially, I had very humble aspirations. My reason for acquiring our first rental property in Florida was to have a home in retirement. I wanted to ensure we had at least one house – bought and paid for – by the time I retired from the JOB world.

It wasn't until I left the Air Force in late 1992 that I started to focus - think seriously - about how to break out of the JOB world. I started to devour books, books about financial independence; books about property investing, books about how to develop a "winning" attitude.

And, then something magical happened. I found myself gaining confidence. I found myself getting up off the couch and taking action. I found myself getting uncomfortable as I ventured out into the world beyond the JOB. Soon, I found myself getting comfortable with my uncomfortableness - so I stretched further. I found myself losing touch with people entrenched in the JOB world. I found myself changing, changing for the better!

I started asking better questions such as:

- *There are people making a very nice living without a job – how do they do it?*

- *There are people making a very nice living at what they love to do – why can't I?*

- *There are people enjoying financial independence right now – why can't I be one of them?*

Once I started asking better questions, my life started getting better.

I began picturing myself as financially independent. I began to see myself as the decision maker, no longer dependent on a company or a boss telling me when I could go on holiday, when I had to be back. I began seeing myself as the person who decided how much I was going to be paid, no longer dependent on the boss or the company to decide how much my service is worth.

I held this picture in my mind. I held it in place even when it seemed fruitless, ridiculous; when it seemed like a waste of time. And, finally, after many years of focus – and working my BUT off – I got there. The vision became reality!

Life without a pay check

Then, I discovered something strange about my transition from the JOB world to financial independence.

It was scary!

Why?

After all those years in the JOB world, I became addicted to the pay check. Just like a crack addict, I was a pay check addict. Couldn't live without my fix; my pay check fix.

I went cold turkey – no tapering off. One fine day in July 2009, I just up and quit my JOB. The pay checks stopped dead.

WORKING MY "BUT" OFF!

Every two weeks I had a look of amazement as I discovered our finances were still solid even though I no longer had a pay check! I was dreading a financial meltdown. After all – how can someone survive financially without a pay check? This was new territory for me! After a year or so I started to relax a bit knowing we were financially strong. After two years I started to forget about the pay check. Now, I can hardly remember what it feels like to be dependent on a pay check!

It's been years since I've touched a pay check and I'm still breathing. I'm still alive. Yes, there is life after a pay check. Life does go on. Life does not stop.

And, what's the best part? Life without a pay check has been very good to me! I feel wealthier now. I feel more confident now. I feel more in control now. I feel happier now.

So, back to the original question, why write this book?

Again I ask, "Why not?" Why not tell others about my transformation? Why not share how I worked my BUT off to overcome my JOB mentality and step into full time property investing? Why not give hope and encouragement to anyone seeking to exit the JOB world? Why not encourage others to get on the path to financial independence? Why not share my personal experience to show others there's no magic, no secret, no special talent required? Why not let others know it can happen for them too ... if they want it, if they want it badly enough?

The main focus of this book is to encourage you to take positive action towards your goals and dreams. Encourage you to take control. Encourage you to go for it.

You can do it!

As such, the book is not a "nuts and bolts" manual. It's not a "how to" book. It's more of a "You can do it" book.

Why omit the "nuts and bolts?" Well, the main reason is there are already so many books available to tell you "how" to become a property investor, books that explain virtually every facet – every detail – of exactly "how" to do it. If you want the information, it's already there. Why should I write another book that just adds to the pile? Why should I write a property investment "how to" book when there are already so many out there that explain it so well, with such authority and with much more subject knowledge than I have?

And, another important reason for leaving out the "nuts and bolts" – this isn't really a book about property investing! It's really about developing the mindset necessary to make a living without a JOB!

JOB Mentality

I'm convinced, if you have a JOB mentality, you can never leave the JOB world! I'm also convinced the JOB mentality brings with it some very financially damaging baggage. Until you offload this baggage, you'll always be in the JOB world; you'll always be thinking JOB. And JOB thinking is broke thinking.

"How so?" you ask.

Well, why is it that some very wealthy professional athletes, movie stars, musicians and lottery winners go broke? Would more money help them? Is that what they need, more money?

I doubt it.

You give them more money, they spend it. And, that's what I mean by a JOB mentality. JOB mentality is "spend" mentality. Earn it, spend it. Earn more, spend more. A never ending pattern that's independent of how much money you make.

Sounds like the government doesn't it? Maybe that's why governments go broke. Maybe that's why more taxes will never be the answer. More taxes, more spending. More spending, more taxes. And, the cycle keeps repeating ...

Thought experiment

Let's do a thought experiment.

Let's give Bob $1,000. His first thoughts, "What can I buy with this money?"

So Bob buys a new sound system for his car – money gone.

Let's give Carl $1,000. Carl's first thoughts, "How can I get this money working for me?"

So Carl buys fifty Christmas trees to sell by the roadside over the holiday break. He sells them all in one weekend, netting a handy

$1,000 profit. He then buys more trees, sells them; makes more profit.

If you worked at the bank and had to give a $1,000 loan to Bob or Carl, who would you choose?

Bob has demonstrated severe JOB mentality leanings. Carl, on the other hand, has demonstrated an entrepreneurial mentality, the mindset of a businessman, the mindset of a wealth creator.

I would happily lend Carl $1,000. As for Bob – I'd ask him to visit another bank!

The idea is to move from JOB mentality – a condition I'm still battling – to wealth mentality! I believe, once that transition takes place – nothing can stop you!

So, instead of writing a property investing "how to" book, I'll stick to cheerleading. I'll stick to helping you get your belief level up, get your belief level on high. Get your belief so high you won't lose focus, so high you won't get side tracked, so high you won't let the "dream stealers" pull you down!

Once you get your belief level up, things start to happen.

Good things!

Focus

Things like focus.

Focus is a very powerful tool. It's in your psychological toolbox; it's in everyone's. Most people never use it. It sits there gathering dust and rust. After a while, most people don't even notice it anymore. It might as well not be there. Never gets used. What a shame. Such a powerful tool rusting away in the bottom corner of the psychological toolbox!

Focus. Focus. Focus. Reach into your psychological tool box and pull out the "FOCUS" tool, then be amazed as the world opens a path for you, the planets align. As you march forward on your quest, watch as people come to your aid, wanting to join your cause, wanting to be part of your fast moving train, wanting to be a part of something that's going somewhere!

Yes, the focus of this book is to motivate you to undertake your life calling, your life quest. It may involve property investing, it may not, doesn't matter. All that matters is you begin. Don't delay. Don't wait for the right time. Don't wait for all the lights to go green. Don't wait for your friends to say it's OK. Don't wait for the government to say it's OK. Don't wait for anyone's permission. You're the boss. You're in charge. You're in control. You take control. You decide. You call the shots.

Working my BUT off!

Now, let's get started. Let me share with you how I worked my BUT off. You see I had a lot of BUT questions ... "But, will it work for me? But, can I do it? But, I don't have any money? But, I don't know how?" And, on and on they went!

I had to get rid of these BUT questions because they would only hold me back. I had to work them off so I could take off, so I could fly. I had to eliminate them in order to become "airborne." I had to say goodbye to them so I could achieve "escape velocity" allowing me to leave the "JOB world gravitational field" and jettison into the "orbit of financial freedom!"

And, I'm here to encourage you. To let you know something very important.

YOU CAN DO IT TOO!

4 BUT, HOW DO I GET MOTIVATED TO BECOME FINANCIALLY INDEPENDENT?

Without motivation, nothing happens. So, in order for something to happen, someone has to get motivated.

It's difficult to get motivated when you don't have to. It's difficult to get all fired up about property investing or starting a business when your situation includes all or some of the following:

> *Good job or career*
> *Free housing*
> *Free meals*
> *Free work uniforms*
> *Free medical and dental care*
> *Free training courses*
> *30 days paid vacation every year*
> *75% university tuition paid*

Dave Ives

50% pay upon retirement in only 20 years' service
Excess cash to buy TV, stereo, car, vacations

And just where do you get all these nice perks? Where do you find such a cushy set-up?

Well, it turns out old Uncle Sam is at it again. You see, this is the deal I had when I joined the United States Air Force back in October 1981.

When my recruiter Tony finished explaining all the pay, perks and benefits, I had two questions.

How come nobody told me about this before?

How soon can I join?

And, here's the clincher - I had no tangible skills to offer! On top of all these perks and benefits, the US Air Force was willing to train me as well!

I was amazed.

What's the catch?

There's always something isn't there? There's always a catch, right?

And, my deal was no exception.

WORKING MY "BUT" OFF!

Yes, the setup was very attractive, but in exchange I had to give up a lot of choices. I had to hand over a lot of decision making to my Uncle – Uncle Sam.

For example, he decided my job. He decided where I would live, what base I'd be assigned. He decided what clothes I'd wear while on duty – military uniforms. He decided what hours I worked, my days off, and my vacations. He could call me in for duty at any time.

For example, I remember, getting off an eight hour shift. It was Friday and my boss called me down to the emergency room.

"Airman Ives, have you got your ambulance license?" Staff Sergeant Nakanishi asked me in her authoritative voice.

"Yes." I replied. Although I'd never driven an ambulance, I had the license. They gave it to me after passing some kind of perfunctory written test.

"Good. This patient needs transport to Letterman. Are you willing to drive the ambulance?" She inquired.

Letterman Army Medical Center is in San Francisco, about 150 kilometers (93 miles) from Sacramento. That's an hour and a half drive if there's no traffic and you know your way.

My thought process was very simple, my boss asked me to do something - I'll do it. As long as it's morally and ethically OK and I'm reasonably sure I can do it, I'll comply. I wasn't into complaining. But, apparently a lot of other folks were.

Dave Ives

"Dave, you amaze me. You just got off shift, it's Friday afternoon, you've been working all week, then I ask you drive the ambulance to Letterman - you won't get back until late tonight - and you say YES! You didn't even put up an argument; you didn't try to get out of it. You just said YES. Crazy!"

So, I got a free trip to San Francisco. Didn't see much, it was dark by the time we hit the city.

The point I'm making here is I was subject to military duty whenever and wherever required. I could have objected about driving the ambulance, but I already knew what would happen – I'd be going anyway. I just saved myself a lot of unnecessary dialog. She had leverage. If I refused to go, she could hurt me. Not physically (although Helen was a pretty tough gal!) but she could mess up my military record with the stroke of a pen.

Yes, Uncle Sam had some serious control over my life, over a lot of my decisions. But that's part of the give and take, part of the trade-offs.

I accepted the trade-offs but not everyone was so thrilled. I remember hearing my counterparts complain – a lot. They weren't as appreciative as I was about living under the following conditions:

<u>Free housing</u> – You live in the dorm with another airman and share a bathroom with the adjoining room. Oh, and by the way, your room is inspected every Monday and any other day the First Sergeant chooses. And, you're subject to all the dorm rules and regulations which can be amazingly silly, defy the laws of common sense. For instance, I got a called in to see the First Sergeant one day. He yelled at me for making him look bad. He was taking a

high ranking officer through the dorm and chose my room because he knew it would be clean. But, I let him down. You see, the room looked immaculate except for one thing. I had one piece of white crinkled up paper lying at the bottom of my trash bin! He chewed me out for it.

<u>Free meals</u> – You're issued a meal card and eat free in the Air Force dining facility. I thought the food was great. But, not everyone agreed with me!

<u>Free work uniforms</u> – Military issue uniforms. Never have to decide what to wear to work each day! Personally, I liked that.

<u>Free Medical Care</u> – Generally this applies only in military hospitals and clinics. I always had decent care but one of my colleagues referred to any military hospital as "The Hobby Shop."

<u>Free Training</u> – Basic Military Training and Technical Schools for your particular job. No nonsense training. I enjoyed my time in Tech School.

<u>30 Days a year paid vacation</u> – If you can get it approved. And, you take it when the work schedule and others with higher priority permit. I felt 30 days paid leave was extremely generous!

<u>50% pay upon retirement in 20 years</u> – As long as you make it to retirement. You may find yourself in the "you're fired" basket at less than 20 years. If so, retirement goes to zero. There have been big drawdowns where good military members are forced out, nothing personal – just business. Still an amazingly generous retirement plan!

Dave Ives

<u>Subject to military living 24/7</u>. This can lead to some ridiculous situations. For instance, I remember walking to work, the 200 yards from my dorm to the hospital where I was assigned as a medic. I saw a lone car pass then stop suddenly with brakes screeching. It backed up rapidly then I saw the passenger window start rolling down as the driver's arm frantically swung the handle. While the window was still making its downward climb, I heard the driver yell, "Get in!" So I did. The yelling continued until I reached the front door of the hospital. I think we travelled a total distance of 50 yards, but the driver managed to pack in a lot of yelling in that time. I just kept repeating the magic military mantra, "Yes sir." Why was the man upset? Because ... I didn't salute his car. I had my head down, thinking about going to work, just waiting for the car to pass so I could make my way across the street. It turns out he was the base commander, highest ranking person on base. He angrily pointed out the big blue flag on the front of the vehicle showing off the eagle – colonel's rank – as he screeched, "How could you not see it?" He was so upset I thought his head was going to explode. I figured this was my last day in the Air Force. After all, I'd committed a terrible transgression - failing to salute an inanimate body of moving metal – the base commander's staff car. After his thirty second tirade, he dropped me off at the hospital front door. The yelling stopped and I never heard anything more. Just another normal day in the military ...

Did I mention good pay?

Well, I thought it was good pay, depends on your definition.

By my definition, it was good pay. The Air Force started me off at $550 per month. To me that was an amazing amount of money, especially since I had virtually no expenses – Uncle Sam was picking up the tab for just about everything! I think the only items I bought regularly were underarm deodorant and toothpaste!

I thought to myself, "Life is good ..."

Good deal – compared to what?

And just why was I so pleased, so happy with my Uncle Sam deal?

Well, let's compare it to my setup just prior to joining the service.

I worked full time at an electronics firm and my take home pay was about $120 each week.

I lived at home, but the arrangement with my Dad was somewhat different, not as sweet as the one with Uncle Sam.

My Dad didn't believe in freeloaders. I paid rent. He lent me money to buy my car – a green Chevy Nova – which I had to repay. Also, he handed me a list of chores to do around the house.

Mowing the lawn was the worst of the chores. Our lawn was big and hilly, a pain to mow. It became my sole responsibility. Before, the task was divided four ways between Dad, my two brothers and me. But, because my brothers were going to college they were exempt. Because I chose to drop out of college I wasn't. I got the job all to myself. My Dad was sending me a message and I was reading it loud and clear. His message was simple and direct,

Dave Ives

"Get out of my house you lazy bum!"

Dad also came up with a creative payment plan for me as follows:

$50 a week for rent

$50 a week for car loan repayment

Now, if my math is correct, that comes to $100 per week. And, going on to more advanced calculations, if we subtract my payments to Dad, I'm left with $20 spending each week.

Oh, by the way, did I mention my car needed gasoline to run? And, yes, gas was a lot cheaper in those days but it still cost at least half of that $20 to keep me going back and forth to work each week.

So, now I'm down to $10 spending money a week. Not a huge amount especially when I had a girlfriend. She was never accused of being a gold-digger!

Keep in mind; this was still a cushy deal. My $50 rent included free meals at home. Also, as long as I placed my dirty clothes in the downstairs laundry basket, Mom would do my laundry.

Yes, even though I was broke – had virtually no spending money – it was still a pretty good setup. But, compared to Uncle Sam's offer, it looked anemic.

Sign me up now!

When Tony, my recruiter, asked when I wanted to go in, I blurted, "Right now!"

He said, "Soonest we can get you in is October. And, that's only if you're willing to go in Open General. Are you willing to go in without a guaranteed job? I wouldn't recommend it."

"How long is the wait if I get a guaranteed job?" I asked.

"You'll have to wait at least six months, probably closer to a year."

Tony gave me the jobs list. I took it home and started to read it. It went on forever, seemed like there was a job for everything - Chief In-Flight Decal Remover, Aircraft Tire Tester Technician, Aerospace Cloud Detection Specialist. I read down until I reached the 50th item or so and quit ... a bunch of mumbo jumbo.

The next day I called Tony.

"Fine, I'll take any job they give me. I want to go in October." I said with relief. I really wanted to go in now, but waiting two months was the best offer he had, so I took it.

A path to wealth?

Was I happy with my Air Force deal?

Yes.

Was I looking at it as a way to build wealth? Not really. But, I sure appreciated it. I couldn't believe Uncle Sam was paying me, training me and providing room, board and all the other benefits. I recognized a good deal when I saw one.

I knew this wasn't a wealth setup. I knew this was great for now, but I had bigger ambitions for later in life.

I was motivated to move forward, to reach higher, and to dream bigger.

I think a lot of my motivation came from feeling like a slacker. I felt like I was not living up to my potential. I felt like I was letting myself down. I knew I was capable of more, so I must do more, deliver more, be more.

Joining the Air Force, I felt like I was going backwards a bit. I'd voluntarily jumped into this hole and now I was clawing my way out. But, it was a comfortable hole for now. Make the most of it. Don't complain, just work. Don't argue, just work. Don't fight it, work with it – make it work.

But, I noticed, not everyone around me felt that way. I noticed a majority of my Air Force co-workers were quite content to curl up and get comfortable with the security of it all. They seemed to be waiting for retirement. They seemed happy to go out and spend all their pay knowing they'd get another dollop at the 1st and 15th of each month.

WORKING MY "BUT" OFF!

My reaction to the Air Force deal was different. I looked at it as a stepping stone, a way for me to "make hay while the sun is shining." In other words, take advantage of all the benefits.

For instance, I could save money. After all, I had virtually no expenses. At home, I couldn't save anything; with Uncle Sam I could pocket almost my whole pay! And, I could take advantage of the education benefits. I could go to school in the evening. Learn a skill or work towards a college diploma. Remember, the Air Force paid 75% tuition.

But, as I observed around me, most of my Air Force counterparts looked at it as a done deal, this is it. They seemed to want to spend all their pay, almost as if there was a penalty for not doing so, as if the next pay check wouldn't come if they didn't spend their current one.

I couldn't relate to this mentality.

I remember one of my co-workers telling how to make the money last until the next pay check. He explained it this way ...

"Dave, we've been in situations where we didn't have any money and we didn't have any food. We were waiting for the first of the month to get paid. So, we'd handle it this way. The wife and I load up the kid in the car and head out to the finest restaurant in town. The maître-d greets us – he knows us by first name – and shows us to our table. It's our special table, overlooking the river; spectacular views of the city. Then I pull out a cigarette and he lights it for me – nothing but first class. My Uncle Neddy always told me, "If you're gonna go – go first class!" Then we order a nice bottle of wine followed by starters then the main course. We top it all off with coffee and dessert. When it's time to pay – no problem - I just get out

the old credit card – it's great! Big meal, downtown, finest restaurant in town and I don't even have any money!

I rattled my head back and forth, not believing what I just heard!

I couldn't relate to spending money I didn't have. I couldn't relate to counting the days, hours and minutes until payday. I would rather go without luxury items – color TV, massive stereo system, eating out, new car, vacation - than go through the financial stress. Yet just about every "payday watcher" had these luxury items! It just didn't make sense to me.

Folks buying things they don't need, to impress people they don't like, with money they don't have.

It's called status and it kills people – financially. It's one of the biggest financial killers out there. Just like there's a warning on cigarette packs, there should be a warning on all credit cards – "This card can kill you – financially. Use it with extreme caution!"

Best benefit of all

It turns out, the best Air Force benefit – perk – of all, came in the form of an orientation class, a mandatory briefing given by the education department explaining basic financial planning. Apparently, a lot of troops were getting into serious money trouble. The problem had become so acute they decided to take action, require all junior military members to attend this financial planning briefing as part of their in-processing checklist.

WORKING MY "BUT" OFF!

I'm so glad! I'm so glad they created the class, so glad they made me attend, so glad I didn't sleep through it.

Once the class ended, my financial motivation level jumped exponentially! My desire to become financially independent took a spike – upwards.

I believe this class was worth millions to me. Better than four years at Harvard Business college. Better than an MBA from Stanford. Better than a lunch date with Donald Trump.

Why?

Because, none of the above can help if a person is not sufficiently motivated!

I'm convinced, there are only two things required to succeed ... at anything. They are as follows:

> *You have to know what you want.*
>
> *Then you have to want it bad.*

How can you get anywhere if you don't know where you're going? You have to have a target.

And the chances of hitting or reaching your target aren't very good if you don't want it bad enough.

If you know what you want but aren't motivated enough to do what it takes to get it, you probably won't!

A business master's degree or meeting up with a master of business can't help when you're not sufficiently focused and motivated.

So, let me repeat the steps required in overcoming the motivation problem – First,

> *You have to know what you want!*

Next,

> *You have to want it ... bad – very bad!*

Yes, I'm convinced, it's not what you know – it's not even who you know – the question is simply this ...

HOW BAD DO YOU WANT IT?

I knew what I wanted – financial independence, financial breathing space, financial freedom.

How bad did I want it?

Well, I thought I wanted it very bad. But, after this Air Force financial planning briefing, my desire took an exponential upturn! If for some reason my motivation wasn't high enough, the Air Force drove it to a stratospheric level. Any defects in my motivation profile were fixed, corrected - they miraculously disappeared.

Thank you Mr. Air Force

I'll be forever in debt to the US Air Force for providing me the motivation I needed to become financially independent.

I'd like to share this story with you. How I turned on my motivation afterburners, how I went from lukewarm to Desert Storm, from subsonic to hypersonic, from "let's be realistic" to "I'm going ballistic!"

I overcame my motivational BUT by listening, listening to someone threaten me, listening to someone try to condemn me to a lifetime of being broke.

Here's the story of how I worked off my motivational BUT!

A Financial Planning Class I'll Never Forget

It was early 1982. I reported to my first Air Force duty station.

I'd been trained as a medic, the guys who run around picking up the wounded from the battlefield. That was my job. But, since there was no war, instead of the battlefield, I was sent to the hospital at Mather, Air Force Base near Sacramento, California.

I was assigned to the medical ward. But, before starting my new "career," I would go through a series of orientation classes.

Out of all these classes I can only remember one, financial planning. And, I remember this class because the instructor said something that frightened me. I'll never forget what he said because it had such an impact, such a shock effect. It frightened me into making my way to financial independence. I wanted to make sure what he said never came true for me. It motivated the socks off me. I never got around to thanking the instructor for his powerful, inspirational, motivational and life-changing talk.

Wow, what a deal!

I sat in the classroom looking around thinking to myself, "Wow! They're going to teach me about financial planning. This is great! I can't believe all the neat stuff the military teaches you. I should have joined up a long time ago. What a good deal!"

I was pretty pleased with my decision to join the Air Force.

I remember back to the conversation I had with my recruiter in Nashua, New Hampshire. "Let me get this straight, you're going to pay me $550 a month, with 30 days paid vacation, free room in the dormitory and a meal ticket?" I repeated back what he told me.

"That's right," said Tony sharply and proudly. "And, remember you get free medical and dental. And, you get free life insurance. Not a bad deal, eh?" he added.

I couldn't believe such a deal! Why didn't anyone tell me about this before? I wanted to sign on right then and there.

WORKING MY "BUT" OFF!

Beats living at home

Of course a deal is only as good as whatever else you're comparing it to.

Well, my "whatever else" was pretty bad. I was working a full time job and couldn't even afford to live at home.

And my Dad wasn't cooperating. He was charging me $50 a week to live in his house. He told me now that I'm out of school, there's no more free ride.

He also had a stack of chores for me to perform. One I particularly didn't like was mowing the lawn. Our lawn was all over the place - hills, bumps, rocks. Behind the house we would tie a rope to the lawnmower handle and drop it down the steep slope to make the cut. It was a pain in the butt.

In the old days my two brothers would help but since I dropped out of college, it was now my job. My brothers no longer had to help because they were still in school. Staying in school had its privileges in Dad's house.

There were other expenses and I wasn't making much money.

Living at home was tough.

Dad let me borrow $1,200 to buy an ugly second hand green Chevy Nova. What a junk box. You turn the wheel and a minute later the car decides to turn. It was the perfect seasickness simulator, had the same ride characteristics as a rowboat in a thunder storm.

He agreed to pretty generous terms; pay him $50 a week until it's all paid back.

Now, here's the rub. I only made a little over $100 a week in net pay. So, after I paid rent and my car payment, I had virtually nothing left over for things like ... gas for the car!

Course, my Dad reminded me of my "good deal."

"How much do you pay for food?" He asked.

"Nothing." I replied.

"So that fifty bucks a week you're paying me covers not just your house but your meals too. Where you gonna find a deal like that?" he questioned.

I stared into space trying to think of a way out of this "good deal."

Course, I knew he was right. Where was I going to find as good a deal as he was offering? That is, until I bumped into the Air Force recruiter!

When the recruiter told me the "Air Force" deal, I wanted in.

When?

Right now! Even if this thing's illegal, I'm in – where do I sign?

Back to the financial planning class ...

The big middle aged man took his place at the front of the class. He was a civilian.

"Good morning. I'm Mr. Teague. I work at the education department here on base."

"Wow, they have an education department?" I thought to myself in amazement. These military guys think of everything. The deal keeps getting better! My eyes got bigger and my attention keener as he started his presentation.

"How many of you here today are single and live in the dormitory?" he asked.

Just about everyone in the class put their hand up. Me too, except I was hesitant to admit "Yes" to his question. Here I was 21 years old – closer to 22 really – single and living in the dormitory with a meal card, totally dependent on the government for my livelihood. Not really bragging rights stuff. Let me tell you a story to highlight what I mean.

Hit to the ego

Just prior to leaving for the military, I visited my old high school and bumped into my former teacher and coach. He was holding soccer practice, yelling out commands and blowing his whistle from time to time.

"Hi Coach." I said with some enthusiasm.

"Hello there Dave, how you been?" he replied politely but gave off the impression that he didn't really want an in-depth answer.

I gave the standard reply, "Fine." And then we stood there for an awkward moment while searching for what to do or say next.

Then I had a thought flash – "I'll tell him about my upcoming Air Force adventure!"

"Did you hear I joined the Air Force?" I asked with an enthusiastic tone. Trying to lift the conversation and get it rolling.

My ploy didn't work.

"Yeah, I heard." coach replied then turned and ran off to talk to some of his players.

That was a blow to my ego. I read into his response. I know you shouldn't "read into a response" but that's what I did. I may have read it all wrong but here's what I came up with ...

He thought I was a loser.

He probably thought to himself ... "Dave was a standout athlete in high school. He lettered in soccer, basketball and baseball. He was voted MVP of the soccer and basketball teams in his senior year. He got good grades. He was a member of the National Honor Society. He was studying Business Administration at the University of New Hampshire. What is this guy doing dropping out and joining the Air Force? Why, what for?"

I remember wanting to chase after him to explain myself. Give him all the reasons why things had not gone according to plan. The disappointments, the trials, all the "feel sorry for me" tales that nobody wants to hear. Thank God I resisted that urge.

Back to the classroom ...

So, when Mr. Teague asked his question about being single and living in the dormitory, I felt a rush of "LOSER" come over me and I remembered my coach.

But, I managed to raise my hand. Yup, I'm one of those guys! Single, living in the dormitory - that's me.

Sometimes the quickest way to move on in life is to admit where you are right now. And if you don't like it, then face it and take action to improve your situation. I was in the mood to take action.

Mr. Teague pointed his finger and then pretended to count the raised hands. "It looks like just about everyone," he said as the final count.

Stand by for some shocking news!

"Well, I'm going to share something with you today. And, if it's the only thing you get out of this lesson, then my talk has been a success." He built up the suspense.

I'd heard that delivery before, great technique for getting audience attention. And, even though I'd heard it before, I was hooked. I wanted to know this critical piece of financial information. I didn't want to miss it. I scooted up in my chair taking a more attentive position.

Mr. Teague continued, "You folks who are single and living in the dormitory, have it made. Let me tell you where you stand financially."

And then he said the phrase that has stuck with me all these years. A phrase that has motivated me financially ever since.

"Right now is the wealthiest you'll ever be in your whole life!"

After he said it, my mind went into overdrive. For the next two minutes I didn't hear another word he said. I was still stuck on this phrase. It kept racing through my mind, generating questions, questions that seemed to have horrible answers or no answers at all. Questions, questions, questions:

> *Ok, I'm making $200 every payday. That's the wealthiest I'll ever be?*
>
> *How come that doesn't sound very wealthy?*
>
> *How come I don't feel wealthy?*
>
> *You mean it gets worse financially from here?*
>
> *You mean I can look forward to a lower standard of living as I get older?*

WORKING MY "BUT" OFF!

You mean I won't be able to live at least as good as Mom and Dad? (Dad makes way more than $200 a pay check)

Is this another way of telling me I'm a loser?

Is this wealth?

When my mind finally drifted back to the classroom, I started to pick up some of Mr. Teague's explanation for his bold statement.

"You have no expenses. Your meals and housing are provided. The only thing you need to buy is toothpaste and underarm deodorant. Heck, you don't even have to buy toilet paper, the dormitory provides that too!"

I listened but what he described didn't sound like "wealth" to me. It sounded like a good deal, a temporary good deal. But, not something you would want for an extended period of time – say a twenty year career. It sounded like a good place to start. But, "the wealthiest you'll ever be in your whole life?" He can't be right. Please tell me he's wrong.

It was too much for me to think about. If this was as good as it was going to get financially, then why bother? I wanted to hop out of my seat, get a running start and dive head first out the window!

Not me!

Then I got angry. "I'll show him. I'll prove him wrong. What he's saying may be true for others but it's not going to be true for me!" I pledged to myself.

I wasn't going to say it out loud for fear of having to defend my challenge.

Yeah, I had doubts. Serious doubts.

And, here's the biggest doubt, *"What if he's right?"*

I tried to erase that question from my mind, too hard to contemplate.

But I made sure I heard my pledge. I was really the only one who needed to hear it anyway. Making my own path in life is something personal, not something I can contract out. It's something I have to do myself. So, why tell anyone else? No need.

At that moment, I made a decision. I decided to prove this man wrong.

After taking this financial planning class, I no longer had a problem getting motivated to achieve financial independence.

I wanted it bad.

So now the question for you is this, "How bad do you want it?"

5 BUT, WHAT IF I'VE GOT A GOOD JOB?

Having a good job is not my idea of a strong income foundation. To me a job is temporary income. It's income that's only two words away from disappearing.

What are these two magic words?

That's right, the Donald Trump battle cry, "You're fired!"

Sometimes it's said in a different way. The phrase can be disguised. But the meaning is the same, the result is the same, the effect is the same.

You no longer have your job!

Some variations used in place of the standard "You're fired" are as follows:

Sorry but we no longer require your services.

You've been a great and loyal worker but unfortunately, your division is disbanding and your job has gone away.

We've had to downsize, and we no longer have any work for you.

The new tax laws require us to downsize, therefore we had to come to the difficult decision to let you go.

The company has entered bankruptcy. As part of the agreement, we have to stop all work. You no longer have a job with us.

We didn't win the follow-on contract. You're free to look for a new job with a new company.

Normally, every job comes equipped with a boss. And if one day your boss decides to mention the two magic words – or one of the alternate phrases - your income takes a big hit. For most people this hit means a 100% loss of income. For most people their job is their only income source. For most people their job is their financial lifeline.

I personally believe having a job as your only income source is scary. To me it's like dangling from a rope 150 feet above the river and having your boss standing over you with a pair of lawn clippers. And, I don't find it the least bit amusing when the clippers snap and I look up to see the rope still intact, then he snickers, "Just kidding!"

Not funny.

I've been there, 100% of my income from a job. I didn't like it. I felt trapped, financially out of control, financially weak. Like a skinny eighty pound weakling scurrying around the weight room handing out towels to big musclebound body builders - nothing but a financial towel boy.

Not a confidence building situation. And after years and years of this conditioning, it's hard to change, hard to see a way out, hard to see it ever ending.

For me, the biggest drawback of a job is the single income stream. You're totally dependent on one source of income. If this one source dries up, your income drops to zero!

Way too risky for my taste!

In a job, you have one customer – your boss. If things don't work out between you and the boss, who do you think ends up with the pink slip?

For some reason we've been tricked into thinking a job is permanent income. Well the secret is out. Tell all your friends. Announce it in the streets. Let the truth be told.

A JOB is not permanent income!

A job is nothing more than a contract from payday to payday. If paydays are two weeks apart, then you have a two week contract. Once you get paid for your hours, the contract is over.

Any company loyalty is a bonus and at the sole discretion of the company. Any promises you get are fluff. Any assurances - merely talk. And, see how many groceries you can buy with fluff and talk!

I learned all these things about a job long before I ever got out of high school. I learned it from my Dad.

Here's the story ...

The Long Ride Home from School

"What a beautiful sunny afternoon." I thought to myself as I waited for my ride home. Mom was going to pick me up from school, kind of a treat because it beats taking the bus and it beats the two mile walk. The bus is not very exciting because we're the last stop, so it seems to take forever. We can get home in about the same time by walking the two miles. So, some days when the weather's nice – like today – my brothers and I just walk home. But, today was different. I was going to get a ride. Nice.

I was almost sixteen years old and in my sophomore year of high school. It was 1976.

When the family car pulled up I noticed something wasn't right. I could sense it. Then I opened the door and looked inside and discovered the problem. It wasn't Mom driving, it was Dad.

"Hi Dad," I sort of asked as if I wasn't sure who I was talking to.

"Why is Dad picking me up at two thirty in the afternoon on a weekday? Isn't he supposed to be at work? Something's up. And by the look on his face, it isn't something good."

As I sat down in the front seat my Dad said abruptly, "Take a look at that letter."

WORKING MY "BUT" OFF!

I looked down and saw the envelope sitting on the front seat between us. It was odd looking mostly because of its color. It was pinkish and looked like one of those letters you get from the Internal Revenue Service saying you owe twenty cents in back taxes from ten years ago and if you don't pay they're going to have the county sheriff on your doorstep within twenty four hours to repossess your home.

I didn't want to open the letter. My Dad looked upset. It could only be bad news.

I stared at the envelope and seriously thought about asking, "Why do you want me to look at the letter? What for?"

Instead, I kept quiet. My Dad was not the kind of guy you questioned. He probably would have taken that simple question as back talk and if so, the conversation could take an ugly turn – against me. So, I resisted and picked up the envelope and pulled out the letter inside.

It was an awkward moment because I soon realized I had no idea what the letter was saying. It was full of double talk and big words that no one ever uses in normal conversation. After reading it I didn't know whether my Dad got a raise or got drafted into the army. I didn't know how to respond, how to explain my lack of understanding, so I just sat there and said nothing.

"Well, what do you think?" my Dad broke the silence.

"Think about what?" I responded.

"The letter!" his tone grew sharper. "What do you make of it?"

"Oh no – Here we go again, another question session with Dad." I thought to myself angrily and a little scared. "Why doesn't he just tell me? Why does he have to draw it out like this?"

Then as I sat there thinking, he blurted out, "I got laid off from my job today."

My initial thought was relief, "Is that all? Big deal. Don't worry about it."

I quickly held that thought inside because I could see it was a very big deal for my Dad. I found out over the course of the next year or so just how big a deal it was to him.

But, from my vantage point, it was just a job. If you lose your job don't you just go out and get another one? Besides my Dad didn't even like his job, he used to complain about it a lot. He'd complain about some of the people, about some of the conditions, about the pay. Heck here's his chance to get out of that situation. Here's a chance to start something new.

Dad was waiting for my response. As he waited, I thought of some possibilities ...

"Wow, I'm sorry to hear that!" or "Great, now you can start that business you've been talking about!" or "Have you got any other job possibilities lined up?" or maybe "Is that good news or bad news?"

WORKING MY "BUT" OFF!

Bottom line – I didn't know what to say. I was striking out, couldn't come up with anything that seemed appropriate or anything that would make the situation better. It was like seeing the next of kin at a funeral – what do you say?

I finally stopped my random thought generator and went with the clunky, unimaginative question that happened to be sitting in the queue, "So, what are you gonna do now?"

Sorry, that's all I could come up with at the time. I was lost. I didn't really want to talk about it. I wanted to talk about baseball – how about the Red Sox? Something sports related, something exciting.

Not job layoffs.

I was in high school. I wanted to talk about how to meet girls. Why couldn't my Dad give me some pointers on how to talk to the girls and get dates? Can't we talk about job layoffs later – much later? How about never?

Then, even before I finished my response, Dad shot out, "I'm gonna find another job, that's what I'm gonna do!"

If he was a weapon he'd have been a machine gun and I would have been full of holes! His response was rapid fire. As if he'd been waiting for me at the pass. Waiting for me to come around the bend and then hit me with everything he had. I could sense his frustration, his feeling of betrayal, his lack of belonging, his sense of being left outside in the cold. He somehow managed to convey all these feelings in his short burst heavy caliber response.

I knew he wasn't upset with me. He was just upset. He was knocked off balance. I could feel his pain all the way over on my side of the car. I tried to push myself closer into the door to escape the negative atmosphere.

The conversation ended. We sat silently for the rest of the ride home.

Dad was a good worker

My Dad was devastated. He couldn't believe the company would lay him off.

I remember Mom telling me about Dad's work ethic.

"He was a good worker. He would get projects done on time – or sooner. He would get projects done on budget – or sometimes under budget."

She continued, "And, he was a conscientious worker. He showed up on time – or earlier. He worked hard. He didn't cut corners. He took pride in his work."

As an electrical engineer with an aerospace engineering firm, he had an interesting and well-paying job. He had a bit of status, worked in a nice office, travelled to major cities for projects and received the respect associated with a professional career.

But, all the while, lurking in the shadows was a creepy fact. Despite all the pay, perks and privilege the reality was this ...

WORKING MY "BUT" OFF!

My Dad had a job!

As such, he was vulnerable. Just like everyone else who has a job. No one escapes it. No matter how much they pay you an hour, you're still in the job world, still bound by the job world rules.

And the rules are set and administered by the company. The rules are executed by the bosses. And, unfortunately, with every job comes a boss. You get one for free, no extra charge.

Apparently, my Dad didn't realize he could be laid off. He didn't realize doing a good job wouldn't save him. He didn't realize it was nothing personal, just business.

He thought the company would keep him on. He thought the company would get rid of all the lazy workers; the non-performers and keep him. He thought the company would hold on to him until new contracts came in.

After all, when times were good, my Dad was making big money for the company. Why would the company abandon him? Wouldn't they retain him until new contracts came in? Wouldn't they share some of the wealth created during the good times?

Nope!

Not gonna happen.

Yes, my Dad was a good worker but the company wasn't going to keep him around if the work dried up. They're not going to pay him out of overhead. Why should they? It's too expensive, too much pressure on the bottom line. Not good for business. Not good for the shareholders.

So, he got the axe - nothing personal, just business.

My Dad could hardly believe it, could hardly accept it.

He was not in a good state of mind to look for a new job. His confidence crumbled. It appeared his self-worth was tied up in his job and now the job was gone.

Not a good situation if you're trying to convince someone to hire you.

It took my Dad nearly a year to find another job. I believe he would have found work a lot sooner if he had not taken the job loss so personally. If he could somehow uncouple his self-worth from his job, I feel he would have been a lot better equipped to "sell himself" to another employer.

And, by uncoupling his self-worth from the job, he would have been in a much better psychological position to strike out and maybe start his own company. Switch from looking for a job, to creating jobs, from working on someone else's dream to creating his own dream, from making someone else wealthy to making himself wealthy.

The layoff had a long lasting effect on my father. Years later I remember Dad saying, "I never recovered financially from getting laid off."

WORKING MY "BUT" OFF!

Yes, my Dad was a conscientious worker but his job wasn't his passion. He didn't speak highly of his job. He especially didn't like the bureaucratic red tape and the office politics.

Then why was his life so dominated by it? Why was his life dominated by something so dreary? Something he positively didn't like and couldn't wait to retire from?

Instead, why wasn't his life dominated by something he loved and truly believed in? Why was my Dad like so many others, clinging for dear life to a job he didn't like?

Why?

How come my Dad wasn't working at something he loved to do?

He loved working on machinery. He loved designing electronic systems. He seemed happiest when rebuilding an engine or wiring a house.

He loved beautifully designed buildings. He loved the science of architecture. Why didn't he have is own business working at something he loved? Is there a law that says your vocation cannot be something you love, something you're good at, something you enjoy doing? The way people flock to jobs they don't like, it makes me wonder …?

I've never forgotten that day – the day my Dad lost his job. It left a big mark on me.

"Why" is more important than "How"

I vowed to never let a job have this much control over my life. I never wanted to be in a situation where my job dominated my life – where it became directly connected to my self-worth.

I knew I had to find a way to uncouple the link between my job and my financial well-being. I knew I had to find a way to make a living without a job.

But how?

The good news is I didn't have to know how.

The first and most important step is to know why. I knew why. I saw my Dad. I saw what the job world did to him. I knew I had to find a way out, an escape route.

Once I knew why, the how would come. It may take a long time, but it would come.

The right vehicle

Did I know it would come via property investing?

No!

But, all through my job career, I kept looking for the way out. I kept looking for a way to become financially independent – independent from a job.

WORKING MY "BUT" OFF!

And because I was looking, I found it.

The key is this ... you got to be looking! How can you expect to find something if you're not even looking for it?

I would contend that most people in the job world are not looking. They are not looking for a way out. Instead, they're looking for ways to go deeper and deeper into the job world.

Get another diploma, work more overtime, take fewer vacations, arrive early, leave late – thinking these rituals will get them ahead. They are trying to achieve employment security, career satisfaction and financial independence via their job.

I would say that's the equivalent of trying cross a torrential river with a bicycle. A bicycle is the wrong vehicle for the job. It won't work. You need to find another vehicle.

What happens when you rise quickly through the company, then one day find an "Out of Business" sign hanging in the parking lot. Gates chained, doors locked.

The company was going bankrupt for years but never told you the real story. They told you all was fine. They even gave you a big bonus. They even gave you a big dinner to celebrate your achievements. But never mentioned they were shutting down. They never told you to prepare financially for the collapse. They never said a word about the coming financial tsunami.

Remember, the company was your vehicle to employment security, career satisfaction and financial independence. Now, your vehicle is sunk. It's at the bottom of the river. It really wasn't designed to get you where you wanted to go. It was advertised as the right vehicle, but it really wasn't.

And, what about all those government workers ... great careers, great pay, rock solid job security and amazing – almost lavish – retirement plans?

Here's something to think about. What happens when the government pay-check stops coming? What happens when the government retirement check stops coming?

Can't happen?

Glad you think so.

Here's the reality. When there's no money – there's no money.

Bottom line - Uncle Scam – oops, I mean Sam - is running out of money. He's trying to stay ahead by printing more. For now, he can get away with it. As long as the world views the US dollar as its standard currency, Uncle can keep printing. But, the minute the world catches onto Uncle's scam – spending more than you earn, promising everyone everything; bailing out the billionaires, taxing the hard working middle class into poverty, recruiting more people onto food stamps and other welfare programs – the games up. Uncle's goose is cooked.

The government pay checks will stop. The government retirement checks will stop. The government handouts will stop.

Does the word "Greece" mean anything to you?

Did I hear you say, "Can't happen in the Good Ole USA!"

Ever heard of Detroit?

Change your thinking

So, you might ask, "What am I supposed to do?"

Good question.

The most important thing I would suggest is this ... you must adjust your thinking and realize a job only provides temporary income. That's the most important thing I took away from my Dad's layoff experience.

It's OK to have a job. But, realize what it is. Don't try to make it into something it isn't. Thinking your job will make you a millionaire is like riding around on a ten speed bike and telling everyone it's a Ferrari. It's not a Ferrari. It's not even a Ford. It's a ten speed bike. Remember that.

And, just because you convince fourteen other people that your ten speed bike is a Ferrari, doesn't change the fact. Just because your fan club agrees with you - says it's a Ferrari - doesn't mean it is one.

Next, you must build your financial wealth outside the job. You can use your job income as seed money, but the wealth will come from outside your job.

I feel it's OK to have a job, OK to look for a job, OK to like or love your job.

What's not OK is this ...

Thinking your job income is permanent income. It's not. You can be fired, let go, made redundant, laid off, furloughed, and terminated at any time - without notice.

Thinking you have a job for life; income for life. It may turn out that you do, but thinking so – believing so, can be hazardous to your financial health. And will probably be hazardous to your psychologically health if – God forbid – you lose your job!

Thinking your job is a path to financial independence; putting all your financial eggs into the company basket. Believing the company is going to take care of you.

On the other hand, a job can be a great way to create seed money necessary to build real wealth. For instance, to build a solid property portfolio that will give you a massive backup income stream – in addition to your active job income!

Also, a job can be a great way to get paid to learn a skill. Then take that skill and spin it into your own business!

A job can be a great place to make new friends and –who knows – maybe even find someone to marry!

A job can be a lot of fun. A place where you earn money, learn new skills and create some awesome lifelong memories!

As long as you're aware of the rules, you should be fine. But, when you start playing the job game by a set of rules that don't match reality, you're in trouble.

And, unfortunately, most people in the job world do this. They think job income is permanent income. They think the company would never let them go. They are playing by a set of rules that don't exist.

Find your vehicle

So, why do I need property investing?

I don't. And, you don't.

But, if you want to achieve a substantial, residual based, backup income, you need something. You need something besides a job. A job won't do it. It won't fit the bill. It's the wrong vehicle.

A job will leave you financially vulnerable and, if that's what you want, if that's what you like – fine. As long as you're aware of the financial dangers associated with a job – any job, regardless of how much or how little the pay and you accept the consequences. That's OK ... your decision, your choice.

I happened to choose property investing because it does fit the bill. It is the right vehicle for the job (no pun intended!)

You may choose something else. But, you must choose something. A job won't cut it.

6 BUT, WHAT IF I FAIL?

I'm still trying to work this BUT off. It's a persistent BUT. It likes to hang around.

Or, should I say, I allow it to hang around.

I need to keep reminding myself that I control my thoughts. Therefore, I can choose to think about what I want. So if I choose to think about failure, it's my fault, it's my decision.

I've heard it said, and it's also been my experience, "What you focus on gets amplified." So, if I focus on failure, guess what gets amplified? If I think about failure enough – focus on it – I'll eventually bring it about.

Then why should I focus on failure? Seems like a losing strategy.

Instead, why not choose to focus on success? Why not choose to think "success thoughts?"

Yes, why not?

How do you look at failure?

But, I've also discovered another way to tackle the dreaded "fear of failure." You see, failure doesn't have to be a bad word. It almost seems society has made it that way. You and I have the choice to accept this notion or we can reject it.

It seems to me, most successful people have rejected the concept that failure is necessarily a bad thing.

Let me explain.

Learning to ride a bicycle

When learning how to ride a bicycle, did you ever fall off? If so, each time you fell off the bike did you consider yourself a failure?

I didn't think so.

Instead, each time you fell off the bike didn't you hop back on and try again? Didn't you look at each fall as a stepping stone to eventually figuring out how to ride properly? Didn't you just view the falls as part of the process?

And, maybe – just maybe – learning to ride the bike – with all the falls and spills – was enjoyable, even fun!

How would you feel if you observed someone learning to ride a bike and they gave up after one fall?

Wouldn't that seem unreasonable? How can you expect to ride correctly the first time? It's highly unlikely. It's doesn't make any sense.

So, it appears the spills and falls associated with learning to ride a bike are all just part of the process. They're expected. They're a rite of passage. They're built in.

Each spill, each crash, each fall, is not considered a failure.

Do you agree?

If so, then why doesn't this same philosophy translate to virtually all new ventures, all new learning experiences?

Why is it if someone starts a small business and it goes under, they call it a failure?

How is that different than falling off the bike?

When you fell off the bike, what did you do?

You got back on.

Using the same approach, when your business falls down, shouldn't you just go out and start another one? Shouldn't you use the experience from the first business to build your next business? Shouldn't you just look at the business collapse as a stepping stone, a lesson, and part of the learning process of how to create and build a profitable business?

WORKING MY "BUT" OFF!

Don't learn to ride near a cliff!

Would you agree it's probably a good idea to stay away from steep cliffs when first leaning to ride a bike? When starting out, maybe you should stick to large flat areas where you can crash in relative safety.

Well, wouldn't that same concept apply to virtually any new venture? Why wouldn't you take that same approach when starting a business? Minimize risk. Stay away from any steep financial cliffs. Why wouldn't you start small, apply training wheels, have someone hold you up and run next to you, have someone give you a push? Then see if you can ride solo. If you fall, get back up and run it again. Keep repeating until you get the hang of it.

The problem with learning to ride a bike next to a cliff is this – one mistake and you're dead. They tell me it's hard to recover from death. Not easy to get back on the bike when you're dead.

Well, let's extend this analogy to starting a business. Would you really want to start a business "next to a cliff?" One mistake and you're financially dead?

Wouldn't it make more sense to minimize risk so that any "failures" are not fatal?

Good news, no fatalities in business!

By the way, it's my belief there are no fatal business failures. As long as you're still alive and breathing, you're still in the game. Yes, your business may be finished, kaput, done, dusted, over, bankrupt, collapsed, doomed, shut down, obliterated, crashed, burned, bombed, drone-striked, overrun, (*your favorite word goes here*!) - but as long as you're still alive, you're in the game - if you want to be.

And there lies the secret. Four simple words – IF YOU WANT TO BE! Remember, you choose your attitude, you choose how you want to look at things, situations; events. You choose to decide if you're defeated or not!

If you think you're defeated – you're right. If you think you're not defeated – again, you're right!

You see, it's all up to you. You're the decision maker. You're the boss. You're in charge, in charge of your thoughts, in charge of your feelings, in charge of your actions, in charge of your life.

Who's afraid of failure?

Ok, I'll admit it – I'm afraid of failure. I'm afraid to fall off "the bike." Especially if there's an audience watching me as I try to figure out how to stay balanced and keep the wheel straight.

I'm afraid to "fail" at business especially if there's a group of people watching and hoping I'll "crash and burn." Ready to walk up to the smoldering ashes and bark out, "I told you it wouldn't work!"

But, here's my challenge - I must get over this fear of failure! I cannot let this fear stop me. Yes, I'm afraid – so what?

WORKING MY "BUT" OFF!

I must somehow look at each failure as simply a stepping stone. Each failure gives me another "course correction." Each failure moves me closer to success. Each failure is a necessary part of the journey to success.

If I can adopt – and hold – this concept of failure, then something magical happens, something mystical, something almost supernatural.

Here's what happens ...

>*Failure is no longer failure.*
>*Failure becomes a "success" ingredient*
>*Failure leads to success*
>*Failure becomes medicine*
>*Failure becomes something I welcome*
>*Failure is my friend*

Taking on this concept of failure leads me to the following conclusion:

>*I need failure in order to succeed!*

In other words, if I focus on avoiding failure, I'm sabotaging my chances of success. If I go through life trying to avoid failure, I will also avoid success. Show me someone who has never failed and I'll show you a failure!

So, the message is clear.

>*Success follows failure.*

Struggle comes before success. I must do the work – and risk failure - before I can feel the joy of success. I must cut and gather the firewood before I can feel the warming heat from the fireplace. I must plant the crop – and risk failure – before I can expect a harvest.

The failure bonus

Aren't the best stories the ones that deal with massive failure? The stories where the hero has to overcome seemingly impossible obstacles and setbacks?

Why is it we tend to be fascinated by the struggle, by the journey? Why is it we sometimes feel the final victory isn't as sweet as the struggle? The final victory is a letdown.

Could it be that all the excitement, joy, fun, adventure of life is contained in the struggle? Could it be that fear, pain, wounds, hurt, and suffering is how you develop mental toughness? Could it be that without struggles, life becomes way too boring? Could it be that adventure and risk taking are good for your overall psychological and physical health? Could it be that failures and struggles are the best medicine for building life coping muscle mass, survival skills, physiological staying power?

Well, it looks like we've discovered the "failure bonus." If you want excitement and adventure, then take on projects where you risk failures along the way. When the failures come, welcome them. Enjoy them. Take them on with courage. Think about how much knowledge, how much wisdom and how much strength you'll gain from the experience. Think about how you'll become a better person by facing and tackling setbacks, struggles and failures. Think of the great stories you'll be able to tell when you're old!

What's your attitude towards failure?

Your attitude towards failure is probably the biggest reason for your success – or lack of it – in life.

Don't take it from me. Take it from one of the richest men in the world. You see, I watched this guy on television many years ago and he gave me a new way of looking at failure.

When discussing failure, he seemed unafraid, unconcerned, unworried. He seemed at ease. The interviewer couldn't shake him. He was solid, confident.

This was new territory for me, a new way of thinking.

You see, the world I lived in was teaching me differently. It was teaching me to avoid failure at all costs. I lived in a world where the mantra was, "Don't make any mistakes!" I lived in a world where people handed out phrases like, "Don't screw it up!" And, they handed them out frequently and generously!

But, as I sat mesmerized by this old man, I caught a glimpse of another way of life, another way of living. He viewed the world from a different perspective. He seemed to be filled with a sense of wonder, a sense of adventure, a calm sense of deep confidence.

So, now I'd like to share that story with you, the interview that changed my idea of failure. I highly recommend you adopt this man's view of failure. I'm still working on it. You see, old habits – old ways of thinking – die hard!

Interview That Changed my Idea of Failure

Many years ago, when I was a young kid growing up in New Hampshire, I watched an interview featuring one of the wealthiest men in the world.

Normally, I wouldn't have been interested but for some reason I was gripped to the television waiting to hear the man answer each question.

He didn't speak English very well and the lady interviewer seemed to be antagonizing him, trying to fluster him, trying to trip him up. But, with each attempt, she looked more and more ridiculous and he looked more and more like a hero.

Every time he spoke, I became further enlightened. He didn't think like everyone else. Here was a man who seemed at ease with himself, a man unhurried and unworried, a man who appeared confident but not arrogant, a man in control of his life and his destiny.

Richest man in the USA

"So, you're the richest man in the USA, according to latest reports. How do you feel about that?" asked the lady interviewer as I flicked through the channels to see if there was anything interesting on TV.

I'm not sure why I stayed on this channel because I wasn't really into business or wealth creation at the time. I was more into sports and action movies. But, I suppose the curiosity of hearing what the "richest man in the USA" had to say got the better of me. I'm glad I listened.

He was a short man. A least he appeared short standing next to the lady interviewer. He was somewhat chubby and had a thick immigrant accent. I'd have to guess he was about fifty five years old. He looked very ordinary. The kind of guy you'd pass on the street and not even give him a second glance. No real outstanding features that would make you say, "Hey, look at that guy! He looks like an important person. He must be a millionaire or something." No. Instead he looked to me like the kind of guy who would drive up when you called a cab.

"I feel very good about myself. But, it has nothing to do with my wealth. I love what I do and I love living in this country. This country has been very good to me and I feel compelled to give something back." The wealthy man replied.

I was having a bit of trouble with his response. "... nothing to do with my wealth." What does he mean by that? Aren't wealth and happiness tied together? How can you have wealth and not be happy? How can you not have wealth and be happy? This was my simple thinking at the time. I wasn't very long in the tooth, wasn't yet aware that there are a lot of wealthy people who aren't very happy.

Growing up with money issues

But, growing up in my family, money was a big issue. Or should I say a big negative issue. I grew up with some very negative ideas about money. I'd hear statements like, "Money doesn't grow on trees!" Or "Do you think I'm made of money?" Or "We can't afford that!"

I remember one of Dad's money saving strategies, straightening out bent nails. We'd place the deformed rejects on the concrete floor and hammer them back semi-straight. Then toss the recycled nails into an old coffee can. We'd have the can filled in no time. Big stash of semi-straight nails ready for re-use. It saved Dad from buying a new box of nails.

He had a special name for these nails. He called them "depression nails" – "... cause that's what we used back in the depression." He'd say.

My Dad talked a lot about the depression. He was born in 1932 right when the down turn was in full swing. He talked about it with a sense of pride. The same sense of pride someone talks about surviving an earthquake, or a hurricane, or a war.

He'd tell us with a twinge of pride how he was born in a "chicken coop." When he'd tell us – and he told us a lot – I would sometimes chuckle under my breath because, let's face it, it's kind of funny. I'm picturing my Dad – this big strong strapping man – lying in a chicken coop with all these screaming chickens running and flying around. In my young mind, it was a funny scene.

"Aren't you supposed to be born in a hospital?" I'd ask my Dad curiously. As if to say, "Are you joking with us, a chicken coop, come on Dad, really?"

He would roar back – again with a twinge of pride, "We couldn't afford no hospital!"

I wanted to continue the questioning but I wouldn't dare. My Dad was more on the serious side than the joking side. He did have his joking moments but it was not easy to tell when that would be. It was safer not to push my luck.

But, if I was braver, I would have continued by asking, "Why couldn't you afford it?" Seemed like a simple situation to me. Just go make some more money. No big deal. Making money is easy right?

But, that thinking got drummed out of my head soon enough. After a while I wouldn't even think to ask such a question. I started to believe that money was HARD to get. And, guess what? I was right. After all, whatever you believe becomes truth – doesn't it? I was forming a truth that was going to make my financial life very difficult.

Be careful what you choose to believe, could mean the difference between an enjoyable life and a miserable life.

The big question

Now, let's get back to the TV interview.

The lady interviewer asked more questions. From these questions we found out the millionaire was not born in the USA. We found out he started off penniless on the streets of New York City. We discovered he didn't show off his wealth but kept to a very simple lifestyle.

The more he talked, the more I got to know him, and the more I came to like him. He had a gravitational pull about him. I wanted to know what he knew. I wanted to learn from him. I wanted to be like him.

Then the lady interviewer asked a particular question. A question that I felt was a bit embarrassing, one that seemed to put the millionaire on the spot.

She asked the question with a hint of arrogance. With a sense that this question would show the world this guy is just like the rest of us. Put him in his place. Bring him down to earth. Knock him down a few notches. I was feeling a bit upset with the interviewer as she asked, "What would you do if you lost everything and had to start all over again?"

I held my breath. What's he going to say to that? She's got him? Here are some of the answers I was expecting:

> *Jump off a high building!*
> *Go off to Burma and become a monk.*

Move in with my broke brother-in-law.
Beg for money.
Get a government job.
Collect the dole.

That's not what my millionaire said. Instead he calmly responded by sharing his experience. He was ready for this question. His whole life prepared him for it.

Serving up the perfect baseball pitch

It almost seemed like the interviewer served up the perfect pitch, right down the center of the plate. Not too high, not too low. Nice and fast. Then the bat comes around perfectly, just the right stance, the right arm motion, the right wrist action. The eyes are following the ball. Then the eyes see the bat and the ball meet - right at the sweet spot. The eyes see the connection. Then both the bat and the ball disappear. No longer in the place the eyes are looking.

But, you can still feel the result, you can still hear the crack of the bat, you can feel the force as the ball is rocketing away. You can still feel the bat swinging around your shoulders. You know it's a home run. You know it's out of the park, over the fence. You haven't looked up yet but you know it.

You can feel it.

You've been waiting for that pitch, training your whole life for it. You want to go out and thank the pitcher, but you're still in the middle of your swing. That'll have to wait.

Then the bat settles still behind you. The swing is over. You look up. You take a moment to locate the ball. Where is it? Your eyes scan the outfield. "There it is." It's still sailing high.

You see the outfielder looking up too. He's not even trying to catch it. You see the fans standing, looking up. They all watch as the ball sails upward. It's a moment frozen in time, a joyous moment, a moment to savor for a lifetime. Then the ball settles gracefully into the upper decks of the ball park.

You take your lap of glory. You run the bases. You touch each base as if it's your best friend. This is your victory celebration. And the fans want to join in with you. They want to savor the moment too. They want to see you run around the bases. They're with you in spirit. At that moment you represent their hopes and dreams.

You'd been training your whole life for that pitch. What a beautiful thing. All the training was worth it. All the pain and suffering, worth it; all the lonely hours swinging the bat, worth it. At that moment you wouldn't want to be anywhere else in the world. You're where you're supposed to be, doing what you're supposed to be doing. "Isn't life great?" You ask yourself with a smile.

I wouldn't know how to answer the big question

Now if I were the batter, I probably would have swung and missed the ball by a mile. Same pitch, different batter.

And if the interviewer asked me the same question, I would have "swung the bat and missed the ball by a mile." I would have given the answers I mentioned above. And that's why she wasn't interviewing me. Why bother?

I would have given the same answer as 90% of the population. You know – the people who work HARD for their money. The people who struggle to survive financially, the people who don't understand how the money economy operates; the ones who cling so tight to the little they have that they thwart all opportunities to break out of the rut. They cling to the security of being just over broke (JOB). They think in terms of scarcity instead of abundance.

I was right there with them. Glad she didn't ask me. I probably would have just quietly walked away.

The millionaire responds

But the interviewer didn't ask me. She asked the millionaire. And he hit a home run – right on the fat part of the bat, out of the park. And his smile after he answered was his home run victory lap. He smiled confidently as the interviewer was tongue tied, jaw hanging in disbelief. Just like the pitcher who threw the perfect pitch to the home run hitter – same expression.

I'll recap what he said. I can't remember the exact words but I'll get the meaning and feeling across. The feeling he left with me was hope and excitement. If this guy can do it, what's my excuse? He took all my excuses away.

"What would I do if I lost everything and had to start all over again?" He repeated back to the interviewer as if to say … "I'm not afraid of your question. Are you sure you're ready for my answer.

And, if I tell you my answer will you even believe me? I'll tell you the truth but I don't know if you're ready for the truth."

It was as if he was warming up in the batter's box. Looking at the pitcher and with his eyes saying, "Go ahead and throw your best pitch, I don't care, I can hit whatever you got. Doesn't matter, I'll hit it. Give it your best shot but the harder you throw it the farther I'm going to hit it."

The interviewer responded with an antagonizing tone. "Yeah, if you lost it all you'd be just like the rest of us. What would you do then? How would you respond to such a tragedy? There's no doubt it would be a big blow to go from riches to nothing, so how would you deal with it?" She pressed him.

Watching this disturbed me. I didn't like the way the interviewer asked this loaded question. It seemed to me like asking a grieving person "How do you feel?" Of course the person feels awful, why ask? It's a bit rude. Same here, if you lost all your riches wouldn't you feel awful? Do you need to ask that question? But I'm so glad she asked it. I was about to witness an interview home run. I was going to watch with glory as the ball sailed out of the ballpark. I was going to celebrate with the millionaire, celebrate his victory lap. She served up the pitch and now the millionaire started his swing.

The millionaire swings the bat

"Ok, I'll tell you." He started to ease into it. The interviewer stared with glowing eyes, ready to pounce if he said anything she could pick apart. She was almost gloating.

"First of all, I'd simply go out and make all my money back again." He stated calmly.

The interviewer quickly pounced on his response because she saw an opening in his logic. "What do you mean make all your money back? How would you do that, you have no money? Remember, I said if you lost it all. That means all your money. So, how could you go and make it all back if you have no money?"

It didn't make any sense to her therefore she was quick to point out his mistake. I'm so glad she kept asking questions because the more she asked the further the ball went out of the ballpark. And, I was getting a lesson on what it means to have a "wealth mentality." He had it. She didn't.

The millionaire asks a question

"Well, what makes you think you need money to make money? Where did you get that idea?" The millionaire put it back to the interviewer. She took the bait.

"Everyone knows you need money to make money! That's common sense." She exclaimed in her excited voice.

"Well, I must not have any common sense, because I don't believe you need money to make money. And, I'm not at the mercy of some silly statement or some silly theory because I have direct experience that says you don't." The millionaire explained.

"What are you talking about?" She replied as if to say, "You better come up with something better or I'll end the interview."

"When I first came to this country, I had no money. I built my wealth starting with no money. I've done it. I could do it again." The millionaire was sharing his hard won experience. Not some theory out of a book. He had done it - hard to argue with that. But, the interviewer continued.

You were just lucky

"Ok, you started with nothing. I'll give you that. But, what if you lost it all today? You're telling me you could just go out and build it all back up again with no money? That's a bit of a stretch. Some people may say you were just lucky the first time. Maybe you just got a lot of lucky breaks. Would you get those lucky breaks again - probably not?"

The interviewer was digging in her heals. But, she was punting. She was now attributing the millionaire's wealth to luck. He was just lucky. She wanted to corner him on this one to show the audience that it all comes down to luck. People with money and success are just lucky. She waited with baited breath for the millionaire to respond. And respond he did!

The millionaire completes his swing

"Funny you should ask if I could do it again." He was now in full swing. The bat was coming around fast and it was about to hit the ball (and the interviewer) with extreme force.

"Because, you see, I've lost everything three times now. And, each time I lost everything I had to start from scratch – no money – and build it all back up again. My wealth today is only from the last five years. Five years ago I was broke. I lost it all. Seven years before that, same thing, I lost it all then built it up again."

I don't remember the interviewer's reaction but I remember mine. I was floored! This guy went broke three times and came back to millionaire status after each fall. Amazing! Unreal! Sensational! Pick a word ... how about "WINNER?" This guy doesn't know how to lose. You can't keep him down.

Ball sails out of the stadium

The interviewer was on her last legs. She gasped for something to ask.

"So, if you lost everything again, you'd just simply go out and build up your wealth again, with no money?"

"That's right. I've done it so many times now I'm getting really good at it. As a matter of fact it takes me less time to build the fortune back now than it used to because I've got a lot more experience. So I don't even worry anymore about losing my fortune because I know I can build it back up in no time." He replied as the ball sailed way over the highest part of the stadium up to the sky and almost seemed to go into orbit.

Victory lap

He then started his victory lap around the bases. He smiled at the interviewer, waiting patiently for the next question.

There wasn't one coming. The interviewer was not pleased. She had the same look as a pitcher who just served up a home run pitch. The same look as the pitcher watching the home run hitter round the bases.

The interview was over. The millionaire tipped his hat to the crowd. I saluted him. Thanks for sharing a new way of thinking. Thanks for letting us know you don't have to go through life broke. Thanks for telling us you don't need to be held back by ignorant sayings like, "It takes money to make money." Thanks for giving us an insight into the millionaire mind, the success driven mind. The mind that says, life is a challenge, get into it. Stop complaining. Stop making excuses. Go forth and make it happen.

Now, I had to ask myself the question ...

What would I do if I lost everything and had to start all over again?

I now had a choice, go with my old answers, my old thinking or, go with the millionaire's answers, the millionaire's thinking?

I chose the millionaire.

And, now I have a question for you –

What would you do if you lost everything and had to start all over again?

7 BUT, HOW DO I GET STARTED?

Getting started in property investing is pretty much like getting started in anything.

"How so?" You ask.

> *Well, how do you get started riding a bike?*
>
> *How do you get started playing basketball?*
>
> *How do you get started playing the guitar?*

In all cases, you have to do it. You have to get on the bike and ride, pick up a basketball and shoot, pick up a guitar and play. At first, you may fall off your bike a lot, you may miss a lot of basketball shots and you may hit a lot of wrong notes on the guitar. But, after a while, you'll be riding smoothly, scoring confidently and playing beautiful melodies – as long as you stick with it.

The key words in the above paragraph are ...

> AS LONG AS YOU STICK WITH IT!

That's the secret. That's the magic formula. That's the way you get good at anything. Show me someone who focuses on a given task for a long period of time and I'll show you a pro at that task.

But, our question is not how you get good at something but how you get started, specifically, how to get started in property investing. So, the same logic applies here. You get started in property investing by simply ...

INVESTING IN PROPERTY!

Now, I can hear you smirking at me saying, "Yeah right, and how do you do that? Just HOW do you get started? How do you get the money? How do know what to do? Who do you talk to first? How do you keep from making a big mistake? There's so much to know, you can't just do it! No way!"

Well, I'm here to say you can.

How do I know?

Because that's how I got started, I just did it. I didn't have a plan. I didn't talk to property experts. I didn't have any idea what I was doing. I just found myself in a situation. An opportunity came up. I grabbed it.

Is this the way I'd recommend you get started?

Not really.

Is this the way to get started?

WORKING MY "BUT" OFF!

Absolutely!

Why?

Because the whole idea is to get started and that's what I did – I got started. Getting started is way more important that getting started correctly. Getting started correctly, or properly, or the right way – is way overrated. It's much more important to simply – GET STARTED. DO IT! AND, DO IT NOW!

And this applies to anything you want to do, anything you want to do well, anything you want to become good at!

So, just "how" do you do it now? How do you get started in property investing?

Well, there are probably as many different ways as there are people on the planet. How did Paul McCartney get started playing the guitar? How did Stephen Spielberg get started making movies? How did David Beckham get started playing soccer?

Although I never asked them, I'll bet it happened something like this ...

Paul McCartney picked up a guitar and started plucking at the strings.

Stephen Spielberg picked up a camera and started taking pictures.

David Beckham started kicking a soccer ball.

That's my theory on how they got started. And, I'll extend my theory to say, at first, they probably weren't very good. But each went on to become a giant in their given profession.

So, if you accept my theory on getting started, then why should property investing be any different?

You get started the same way – go out and make your first property investment!

What's the best way?

Any-way, as long as you start. The only way you can have a bad start is to ... not get started!

Your way of getting started will be different than mine. It will be different from everyone else.

Why?

Because you are unique, you're different, your situation is different. But, it doesn't matter. Your job is to get started. Your job is to figure out first, why you want to do it. Then, once you know why, the how will become apparent – obvious.

Once you make a decision to get started, nothing can stop you.

So, all you really have to do is make a decision to invest in property and you'll figure out how pretty easily. You may make mistakes as you roll down the launching dock, but you'll be in the water. You'll have started your journey. And, that step alone will put you miles ahead of all the other souls who just sit on the shore and dream of all the adventures that lie beyond the horizon!

How I got started

So, you may be wondering how I got started in property investing. What's my story? Was it earth shattering? Was it pure adventure? Was it exciting? Was it exhilarating? Was it high finance at its best? Was it a story for the ages?

I'm happy to report ... "NO"- on all counts! My start was ridiculous. My start was accidental. My start was one I wouldn't recommend to anyone. My start was pure comedy. Not much to see here. No high finance. No savvy strategy. No plan.

Actually, my plan was to not get started. I resisted. I didn't want to get started. But for some reason I did. And, I'm glad.

It wasn't much, but it was my start. The minute I completed the deal, my ship launched. I was floating. I was in the game. I was on the playing field. I was no longer a spectator. I put myself in a position to fail. At the same time, I put myself in a position to succeed. As a spectator, you can't fail. Conversely, as a spectator you can't succeed either. You can only watch.

Once I got started in property investing, I stopped watching and started playing. It's much more fun to play.

And now, here's my story, how I got started in property investing. Hope you're not too underwhelmed!

Dave Ives

Want to go to Florida for the Weekend?

"Hey Dave, we're going to Florida this weekend. Wanna go?" my Mom half-jokingly yelled out.

I had just arrived home on military leave and was looking forward to a little rest and relaxation. I didn't really want to go anywhere, but I played along saying, "Sure, when do we leave?"

"Your Dad and I are leaving on Friday. For a hundred bucks they're going to fly us to Orlando, pick us up at the airport then drive us to the hotel and then wine and dine us all weekend. All we have to do is look at some land they have for sale. What a deal. It's only a hundred bucks, why don't you come with us?" Mom was selling me.

"Only a hundred bucks? They're paying for the hotel? Really?" I questioned.

My mother went on to explain, "Yeah, and they're picking up our meals too. They want us to buy land. But, you don't have to. We don't have any intentions of buying any land, but a weekend in Florida for a hundred bucks is too good to pass up. You should come. I'll call right now and get you a ticket."

I was caught up in the excitement. "I'm going. Book me."

Did you buy land?

By Monday morning we were back in New Hampshire and Mom, Dad and I were proud Florida land owners! I kept joking with Mom and Dad about the salesmanship – by the time Sunday afternoon came around, I would have bought anything these guys were selling!

I had no idea what I was doing but that's how I got started in real estate. Turns out it was a good financial move. I could have said "Thanks for the great weekend, but no thanks to the land offer." And I would have had a great weekend but that would have been the end of the deal. But, instead, by saying "Yes" to the deal, I'm still benefiting from that fun filled essentially all expenses paid weekend in Florida.

Should you go to Florida this weekend and buy land?

Am I telling you to run off to Florida this weekend and buy land?

No.

But, I am telling you my simple story about how I got started in real estate.

Is it high finance wheeling and dealing?

Absolutely not.

Is it years spent in Harvard Business School studying the history of real estate throughout the ages?

No.

It was a small itty-bitty opportunity and my willingness to grab it.

Was it a good deal at the time?

I wouldn't say so.

But, was it a good deal over time?

Definitely.

That's one of the big secret benefits of real estate that I've found – it's very forgiving. If you are patient, you'll win eventually. But, if you're jittery – like the person who digs up the planted seeds before they've been given a chance to grow – you can lose your shirt.

So let's hear the details

My mother was in real estate in 1984 when I went home to visit. She was selling houses in our small town in New Hampshire (NH). The trip to Florida deal came about because a big NH developer was working a real estate project in Citrus County Florida. My Mom and Dad only wanted to go for the "free" weekend. I don't believe they had any interest in getting land in Florida.

After arriving at the Orlando airport, we were greeted by our sales staff, loaded up in the van and headed westward towards the Gulf of Mexico. The journey ended about nineteen miles from the coast where we got settled into our hotel.

WORKING MY "BUT" OFF!

The hotel was very charming. Nice old style architecture with very glamorous looking furniture and large windows. I felt like the clock jumped back about a hundred years to a time when folks were a bit more relaxed and they enjoyed the finer things in life. I was impressed.

We went to our rooms and freshened up and a few hours later were whisked off to a lovely dinner at the development site restaurant. It was here that I received the best after dinner speech I've ever heard. It was given by Mitch, our salesman host, who said, "Waiter, bring me the check!"

Saturday morning we woke up at a leisurely hour and had a beautiful breakfast. Mitch joined us for a coffee and then took us in his big car for a look at the properties for sale. This is when the doubts started to kick in. I thought to myself, "Mitch better be one hellava salesman to market this stuff."

As Mitch toured us around we couldn't help but notice all the sandy lots. I thought Florida was supposed to be green and under water. But all I could see was big dry sandy lots with roads running at square angles.

"Can you picture what this place will be like in ten years?" Mitch tried to create a positive image for us.

"Yeah, sure. It'll look like a giant golf course – the only one in the world that's all sand traps!" I pondered sarcastically to myself.

Mitch carried on without skipping a beat, "With houses on all these lots. Beautifully landscaped ... Can you see yourself owning one of them? And, of course you'll have bought when the prices were low. The folks who wait will be paying top dollar!"

I listened and wanted to believe but it was hard. I'm not much of a green thumb but it looked to me like you couldn't even grow noxious weeds on this land. It looked like desert to me. I was imagining myself buying a lot and then showing people back home the pictures of my astute new real estate acquisition. They'd look at me like I lost my marbles, "You paid money for that?" Then, I snapped out of it and realized I didn't have to buy anything. "This is just a weekend lark. Don't worry about buying any land." I told myself.

Mitch showed us a couple of one acre lots in the lower priced areas and recommended them as perfect for our needs. I'm not sure what our "needs" were, but he seemed to know. I suppose that's what makes someone good at sales – they should help their customer come to the right buying conclusion. Some sales folks are too pushy. We all know that doesn't work. Some back off too quickly – that can be just as disastrous. Mitch was striking a nice balance.

Let's pause to talk about this balance for a moment then we'll come back to the one acre lots.

Pushy salesperson

The pushy sales person may win the battle but usually loses the war. We all know the type; they want to sell you something no matter what. They drive a hard bargain and won't take no for an answer. The problem is the customer leaves feeling bad about the transaction – whether they bought or not. Leaving customers with a bad feeling is not good business – do you agree?

How can anything good come from this type of interaction? Even if the customer made a good purchase, do they want to do business with this sales person again? I doubt it. And, worse yet, what if it's a bad deal?

You get the idea. Common sense says it is bad business practice to be a pushy salesperson.

Pushover salesperson

The pushover salesperson can be just as disastrous as the pushy type.

"How so?" you ask.

Well, if the deal is bad and the customer doesn't buy, then all's well. The pushover won't talk you into it.

But what if the deal is good?

Again, the pushover won't help you make the correct buying decision and you may miss the deal.

How can that be good for you?

How is the salesperson doing you a favor by not assisting you in making the right decision?

They're not. They're doing you a disservice and one that could ultimately lose you lots of money. Let me give you an example.

<u>Setting</u>: 1998 Los Angeles (LA) California. I'm traveling through on business.

"I can't believe the house prices in LA." I said with a sigh.

"Yeah, they're outrageous. I'm glad we bought years ago. We could never afford the house we're living in now if we had to buy it today," said the payroll lady with an excited spring in her voice.

I was traveling through LA and, as usual, I'd been checking out the real estate market.

Just then another lady popped through an open door. She overheard our discussion and wanted in. Without any introduction, she launched into her story.

"Back in the early sixties, my husband came home one day and told me they were selling lots in Manhattan Beach for $5,000. He was all excited and was even talking about buying two of them. Before he could get another word out of his mouth I told him - *Who in their right mind would pay $5,000 for a lot in Manhattan Beach?* My husband has never let me forget those words. Lots in Manhattan Beach are going for nearly half a million bucks today!"

She talked her husband out of the deal.

Did they make a bad buying decision? I think most people (even the couple above) would say, "Yes!"

Who would you rather have in a situation like this, 1) An enthusiastic, knowledgeable and assertive (not aggressive) sales person to assist you in making the correct buying decision or 2) A pushover sales person who just lets you make the wrong decision?

Your call.

Back to the one acre lots...

Mitch stopped the car right in front of a nice patch of sand ... oops, I mean land. Mom, Dad and I got out of the car and walked slowly around the sand bar. I dragged my feet across the ground and let the sand fall all over my sneakers. It was fairly entertaining for me to contemplate how silly it would be to buy any property on offer here. Then Mitch started to ask questions.

"If this was your lot, where would you put your house? Would you go for a three bedroom or would two bedrooms be enough?

I just listened. No answers from me. Remember, I wasn't buying. But, Mom and Dad were polite enough to entertain his questions.

"Oh, we'd probably just get the land and not worry about a house until later on down the track." Mom said offhandedly.

"That's right, not ready for a house just yet." Dad chimed in.

I was listening and these remarks were working on me and working in Mitch's favor. "Sounds like Mom and Dad are thinking about buying some land." I surmised. "No they can't be – who would buy this stuff? They're too smart for that. But, if they want to get some land, maybe I should too? Well, doesn't matter anyway, I don't have the money. If they want to get something, that's their business. I'm staying out of it."

I remember having flashes of how cool it would be to own a piece of land. Then I would own something tangible, a place to build a house someday.

"But, here in this sandlot - I don't think so!"

That Saturday evening we went out for a wonderful dinner at Andre's, the development site restaurant, and had a dreamy meal.

Mitch picked up the tab again.

I was impressed again. Have you ever noticed how food and drink taste just that little bit nicer when someone else is paying?

I was beside myself, because normally, I'd never go out to a nice dinner – too much money. I was making about $220 every half month as an Air Force "two striper." Granted, I lived in the barracks and had a meal card, so my expenses were very low. But still, there probably weren't many people around who would consider that a big pay check. So, things like nice dinners out on the town were few and far between and I certainly appreciated being "treated." His hospitality put me in the mood to listen.

We sat around the table after the meal and talked.

"Can you picture yourself with a nice three bedroom home, beautifully landscaped gardens and sitting by the pool relaxing? The words rolled off Mitch's silk-like tongue.

Yes, I liked that picture. Yes, I wanted that.

"You folks are interested in value right?" We just sat there silently with blank expressions waiting for him to continue. (Is there any other answer but, "Yes?")

"Well, you won't find better prices than what you'll get down here. Both land and building costs are near the lowest in the nation. You'll get a lot more for your money down here. Is value for money a priority for you?"

By the time we finished our discussion, I'd mentally bought the land. The only thing saving me was I didn't have the $1,200 down payment. So, I thought I was free and clear of having to make a tough decision. It's easy - no money, no land.

Paperwork is ready

The next morning we rose from a restful sleep and after another enjoyable breakfast, headed over to the sales office. I wasn't sure why we were there because I wasn't going to buy anything. Maybe Mom and Dad were going to buy. Anyway, we were seated around a table and Mitch came in smiling with paperwork in his hand.

"Morning folks, I've got all the paperwork ready. All we have to do is get it completed and the one acre lots are yours. Just check to make sure the lots are the same ones we looked at yesterday, the ones on East Connecticut Lane."

I was a bit puzzled at the way this discussion was heading. It looked as if we were going to buy this land. I suppose last night we'd given the impression we were interested but I don't remember anyone saying, "OK, organize the paperwork and we'll sign in the morning." I spoke up to get a little clarification.

"Mitch, I can't buy the lot right now because I don't have the down payment." I thought I had him in checkmate. He isn't going to put up the down payment for me so, I'm safe. No sale today partner.

Mitch was no slouch. He didn't argue or say I was wrong or any of the typical responses I expected. Instead, he answered as follows:

"I'm really sorry to hear that, because you're going to miss out on a great deal. The prices of these lots are just going to go up. By the time you do have the down payment, the prices may go up to where you'll have to pay double or even triple what we're asking for them today. But, I understand. If you don't have the down payment, then you can't do it. Lucky for me these lots are selling like hotcakes, so it certainly won't be a problem for me to sell this lot I've got saved for you."

Boy did that speech take the air out of my tires. Now I wanted the land more than ever! Mitch's low-key response also grabbed Mom and Dad's attention. I think they were hooked as well. They didn't want to miss a good deal.

The land was selling for just over $11,000 for each one acre block. For $11,000, I could have my own one acre block of land. And, even to me, this seemed like an amount of money I could handle given the fifteen year payment plan they were offering.

Mom saves the day

I really wanted to buy but was at a standstill until I heard my Mom offer a solution.

"I'll lend you the down payment." She said quickly as if it was an order and I was not to question it.

"Are you sure Mom?" I replied even though I wasn't supposed to. I didn't want to borrow money from my parents but this seemed like a good time to put that rule on hold. I waited for her response.

There was almost no pause or hesitation as my mother answered my probing question. But, there was a fraction of a moment where I had enough time to mentally flinch as I hoped for a positive response. Her response would set the tone. Would she lift me up or make me feel like a small kid who needed Mommy's help? I was 23 years old and did not like the idea that I needed Mom and Dad to make this purchase. I was very concerned about saving face in front of Mitch. But, the moment ended quickly as I heard her beautiful words ...

"Come on Dave, it's only twelve hundred bucks and you'll pay me back right?"

I repeated her words in my mind "...you'll pay me back right?"

Of course! You're right Mom. It's no big deal. I'll pay you back. It's not a problem.

The way she said it was magic. Her words and tone together conveyed to me her belief, her belief that I would pay her back, her belief that I should get this property, her belief that it's right to let me borrow the money.

She did not doubt me and that was probably one of the best gifts she could give me – her belief and trust in me. That's a powerful gift and one that I cherish more than any material gift. I try to keep this in mind as I raise my own children.

Land owner

I signed my paperwork and Mom and Dad signed theirs. We bought. The deal was done. I owned a one acre lot and Mom and Dad owned one too.

The lots were right next to each other. We were sand ... I mean LAND, neighbors. We pushed our chairs away from the table and stood up as proud new property owners. This concluded my first real estate transaction.

My property investment journey had begun. I had stepped onto the field. I was no longer a spectator. I was in the game.

8 BUT, WHAT IF I CAN'T EVEN GET A LOAN FOR A MOBILE HOME?

Getting turned down for a loan is something everyone should experience. And the more ridiculous the rejection, the better! It just makes you stronger. It just makes you more determined. It provides you with a good story to tell your grandkids.

My loan rejection story is pretty high up on the ridiculous scale. I applied for a measly $11,000 loan to buy a used mobile home and the bank said, "NO!"

I had plenty of income, plenty of savings, and paid my bills. But the bank still said, "NO!"

I was a captain in the Air Force making about $38,000 per year with pay and allowances. I had over $10,000 in my savings account. I paid my bills on time.

The bank still rejected me.

Apparently, there was something sticking out on my credit report that gave the bank concern. Enough concern to say "NO DEAL!"

Can you say credit report?

It was at this point that I learned about the all-important credit report. I learned more about this document than I ever wanted to know. So, getting turned down for a small mobile home loan gave me a lesson, a lesson in how to obtain, how to read and how to – more or less - understand a credit report!

Without getting turned down for this loan, I never would have learned how to decipher this incredibly boring document!

The ridiculous part of the whole episode is my credit was outstanding. I didn't owe any money to anyone. All my loans were paid off. My $10,000 loan for an acre of land in Florida – paid off. My $8,000 car loan – paid off. My student loan for $5,000 – paid off.

Nothing owed; clean credit slate.

That was the reality. But, that's not what the credit report showed.

And, it turns out, reality doesn't matter – what matters is what the credit report says. If the credit report says I have two heads and a tail, then that becomes reality ... at least for the person reading the report.

This all important document – my credit report – existed and I didn't even know it. I'd never seen it. People were allowed to add things to it without my knowledge. Is the added information correct? Does anyone verify it? Is there a check in place to make sure the information reflects reality?

No.

Why?

Because that's how the system works!

What if a credit situation changes? What if a misunderstanding has been corrected and both parties are happy? Does the credit report get changed to reflect this new status?

I learned the answer to this question the hard way. As you can probably guess, bad news information gets added quickly but good news credit reporting seems to take a back seat, gets left for last or doesn't get reported at all.

I also learned another frustrating lesson – the credit report information is incredibly difficult to get corrected. I had virtually no control over the process. All the power to change an entry lies with the person or agency that made the original complaint. It's up to them to make the change – or not make the change. And, I found out, even if they agree to the change, I still had to somehow convince them to go through the process – do the work – required to change it! I would have done it, but I couldn't. I wasn't allowed. The credit report agency would only take instructions from the person or company who filed the complaint, in my case - the bank.

But, the bottom line is this ... if you get turned down for a loan – SO WHAT? Doesn't matter, move on.

My reaction was a bit different. My reaction reflected my inexperience. My reaction is not recommended.

You see, when I got rejected for the loan, I focused on getting the credit report fixed. And, after months and months, I did it. My credit report was clean – it reflected reality. It no longer contained the misinformation, the black mark suggesting I may be a credit risk. That information was now gone. I'd convinced the bank to pick up the phone or write the letter or whatever it takes to tell the credit reporting agencies to take it off my report. It took a while, but I got there.

But, here's the problem. While I was focused on getting my credit report cleaned up, I stopped all progress on getting the mobile home. I stopped all progress in looking for alternate ways to make the deal happen. I lost focus on the goal and shifted all my focus to this side issue – fixing the credit report.

Yes, I had to fix the credit report. But at the same time I could have been looking at other ways of making the mobile home deal work. I could have been talking to the bank and explaining the situation. I could have been building a relationship with the bank, show them my savings; show them my pay statements. Maybe look at asking for a smaller loan amount.

Hey, maybe talk to the seller about a cash deal!

I didn't.

Instead, I shifted all focus to getting my credit report corrected. Consequently, I made no progress in securing the mobile home deal or any other property deal.

At first I thought this was a good thing. At first I thought getting turned down for this loan saved me from making a mistake and buying that mobile home.

Looking back, I now feel otherwise. I should have aggressively continued after the mobile home purchase. It made financial sense. It would have given us a tremendous financial kick start. It would probably have allowed us to get into property investment sooner.

But, that's not what happened.

Here's the story of how I got turned down for a small $11,000 loan to buy a mobile home.

Mobile Home – No Loan!

We just arrived in Ohio from an overseas assignment and started looking for a place to live. It was June 1991. Marieta and I had been married for over seven months and we had a child on the way, baby due in November. We had met and married in Australia and now we were starting our new adventure in the USA. We were staying on Wright-Patterson Air Force Base near Dayton, Ohio at the temporary living quarters, affectionately known as the TLQ.

Welcome to the TLQ

I think the TLQs were home hunting accelerators. One or two days in the TLQ and you became focused, motivated - desperate - to find a home!

The accommodation consisted of one long slender room. Half way into the long room was a small half wall marking off the beginning of the bedroom. All the way to the back on the left was the small bathroom.

What I remember most about the TLQ is the air-conditioner. It had two settings – on or off. When turned on, it converted our little room from a steamy heat bath into a freezing meat locker! Also, it seemed to have uneven cooling qualities, leaving pockets of the room still hot while other areas formed icicles. I remember lying on the bed feeling hot and then sitting up and getting hit with a freezing Arctic front! I went from the baking hot Mohave to the frozen Alaskan tundra by shifting my body a few feet! In the end, we'd run the air conditioner until we started freezing, then turn it off. Within a short time, the temperature climbed to "hot and humid" and we'd turn it back on again! I never really felt comfortable or relaxed while staying in the TLQ.

For me the situation wasn't too bad. After all, I got up each day and went to a comfortable temperature controlled office. Not so for

Marieta – several months pregnant – she was stuck in the "temperature challenged" TLQ essentially all day!

The other thing I remember is the price – $25 a day to stay in this uncomfortable room. I wouldn't have minded so much if the government was paying but they weren't, it was coming out of my pocket.

Now, I have to admit, this was a pretty good deal from a price and convenience vantage point. Compared to a hotel, we were saving a lot of money. Also, the TLQ had kitchen facilities and was located on the base making it very convenient for getting to work and shopping.

But, after three days or so, the good deal started to wear thin. We were anxious to get out from underneath it. I could easily find a nice comfortable rental in the mid $500 per month range. When you add the cost of utilities and other expenses, it would probably come out to about $25 a day – maybe a little less. But, it would be a lot more comfortable than the TLQ! We were motivated. We were looking. We wanted to get the TLQ experience behind us – quickly!

House prices too high!

We seriously looked at buying a house but that option fell by the wayside.

I was now a Captain in the Air Force and felt my pay was quite good. But while I was away from Dayton for the past four years something happened that took me by surprise – the price of homes went up faster than my pay? I was shocked. That was a painful real world "ah-hah" moment in my property investment career.

Lesson learned – my pay doesn't keep up with the rising cost of housing!

We were looking at about $80-100,000 to get a three bedroom modest home in Dayton. I thought that was outrageous. So I tried to make an end run – somehow solve the high property price problem – but as you'll find out, that failed.

I got it; we'll buy a mobile home!

My next plan of attack – my end run – was to purchase a mobile home from one of my co-workers. I'd been out to visit him and his family a few times and they kind of sold me on the mobile home concept.

First, it was cheap, only $11,000. I could almost pay cash for it. Next, the government would pay me full housing allowance even though I would probably only need a fraction of it to pay the lot fee. And since the lot was on base, I wouldn't have to pay local property tax. I was excited. I saw a way to have a place to live and make some money as well.

Not everybody was happy with my idea.

Marieta was not excited about the prospects of living in a mobile home. She wasn't thrilled about the neighborhood. It looked ... shall we say, untidy, lived-in, rustic ...? Seemed like a circus camp – ready to pack up and leave at a moment's notice! She also wasn't thrilled with the idea of living in something that didn't feel like a real house. To her, it was like moving into the TLQ – permanently! But, she was willing to go along with my crazy idea if it meant we could save some money and then get something nicer in a year or so.

When I told my Dad about the mobile home, I had to wait several minutes for him to stop laughing. His line of questioning was fairly direct, "What-a-ya doin that for?" I carried on about how it would work out very well for our household bottom line and how it would allow us to save for a nice home later on.

He wasn't moved. He wasn't interested.

When I finished my detailed explanation he just repeated his earlier question, "What-a-ya doin that for?"

Bottom line – whatever I said, my Dad was not going to give his blessing. He was not going to back me on buying a mobile home.

I got off the phone feeling pretty bad. "My Dad thinks I'm a loser for wanting to buy and live in a mobile home," I thought.

Well, it turns out he didn't have to worry because a small hiccup in my past prevented the deal from going through anyway.

Rejected!

So, next step, I went to the bank and applied for an $11,000 loan to buy the mobile home. A few days later I got the news – "not approved." I was amazed! I had nearly the whole amount in my bank account but I didn't want to run my savings dry buying the mobile home. So, I figured I'd get a loan and then pay it off in maybe six to eight months.

But the bank rejected me.

"Sorry Mr. Ives, you have something on your credit report that caused us to turn you down for the loan." said the bank representative in a pleasant voice over the phone.

"Really, what is it?" I asked in a surprised, unbelieving – stunned – manner.

And, then came one of the most amazing and unexpected responses I've ever heard, "I can't tell you."

"You can't tell me ..." I repeated back slowly letting my confusion ooze through the phone line. "How am I supposed to find out? How do I get this fixed?" I continued.

"Well, you can request a copy of the report. That's all I can recommend." She told me.

When I finally figured out how to order the report and eventually received it, I still had no idea why I got turned down for the loan – I didn't know how to read the report!

Somehow I managed to find someone who could help me understand the mysterious coding in the credit report. It turns out the black mark was against my $5,000 student loan – the one that was completely repaid - I owed nothing on it!

WORKING MY "BUT" OFF!

The loan showed up on my credit report as going unpaid for 120 days. Apparently, this is a big credit "no-no" - a loan stopping "no-no."

At first I had no idea how this applied to me. I paid the loan off essentially straight away. I received the letter from the bank saying I had to start making payments. But, instead of making payments, I just paid the whole thing off in one check!

So, how could there be any black mark against this loan? It didn't make any sense.

Well, it turns out something did happen, a small misunderstanding, something we easily sorted out. After sorting it with the bank, I thought we were good. Apparently, we weren't. Instead, the bank loaded up a black mark on my credit report – without my knowing it – and it sat there like a ticking time-bomb just waiting for me to apply for a loan ... then it exploded!

Here's what happened.

I took out a $5,000 loan while attending college, mostly, because the other guys were doing it to buy fancy computers. So I jumped on the bandwagon.

After graduation the loan payments were supposed to start. But, I was off to officer training school in San Antonio, Texas and then – 90 days later following graduation – off to my first duty assignment in Denver, Colorado as a brand new 2nd Lieutenant.

Dave Ives

About six months into my Denver assignment I received a letter from the bank saying my student loan repayments were overdue. I immediately called the bank and explained my situation.

"I just received your letter today. I didn't realize these payments were overdue. This is the first noticed I've received." I told the bank representative.

I continued, "I spent 90 days in San Antonio for officer training school and then moved to Denver where I'm stationed. I suppose it's taken a while for my mail to catch up with me. Like I said, this letter is the first I've heard about repaying the loan."

"There's nothing to worry about Mr. Ives. Now that you've explained the situation, there's no problem," replied the bank representative in a refreshing and reassuring manner.

And, more good news, "Since you're in the military, your repayments are deferred for two years. Just make sure we have your correct address and we'll send out another letter letting you know when it's time to start making repayments. In the meantime, you've got nothing to worry about."

I hung up the phone thinking ... "That was a good conversation!"

Two years later I received a letter from the bank saying it was time to start paying back the loan. I wrote a check for $5,000 and mailed it to the bank. The debt was cleared.

WORKING MY "BUT" OFF!

Black mark!

But the damage to my credit rating had already been done. After my graduation from Ohio State, the bank expected me to start making re-payments. I didn't know this, I didn't receive any notification. After 120 days, the bank called the credit report agency and said, "Black Mark this guy!" Seems the bank was very efficient at entering the black mark.

Too bad they weren't as efficient at taking it off!

After all, I was never late on any payments. Not 120 days, not 90 days, not 60 days, not 30 days, not even one day! Remember, I had a two year military deferment!

So, here's my question, after I talked to the bank representative on the phone, why didn't the bank immediately call the credit reporting agency and promptly ask for the previous black mark to be removed?

Did they just forget? Was it not in the bank book of procedures? Was it too much trouble?

And, why didn't I ask them to do it? Why didn't I follow up to make sure they did it?

Answer: I didn't know it was there! I didn't even know the black mark existed! How was I supposed to know to ask them to take it off when I didn't even know it was there?

Crazy system! Crazy was of doing business! Crazy!

A few more questions as follows:

> *How come the bank can just call up the credit reporting agency and say "black mark him" and the agency does it – no questions asked?*
>
> *How come the credit reporting agency doesn't ask for proof before complying with a "black mark" request?*
>
> *How come I wasn't notified a "black mark" was going on my credit report for the entire world to see?*
>
> *How come the bank is so efficient, diligent, and militant when it comes to handing out a "black mark" but when it comes to removing a "black mark" they seem uncaring, unknowing and unconscious?*

I found this whole situation disturbing.

But, it also stopped me from buying the mobile home.

No deal!

Once the bank told me the bad news, I notified my coworker, "The deal's off. The bank turned me down for a loan."

He looked at me like I had two heads, "What do you mean the bank turned you down? It's only $11,000. We're not talking a lot of money here!"

He gave me the same look the teacher gives a second grade student who says, "The dog ate my homework!"

His wife was even more doubtful. The feeling I got from her was this - I was backing out of the deal, simple as that. One excuse is as good as another if you want to back out!   She didn't really believe my story, silently conveying this message: "You expect me to believe that? Yeah right!"

On the other hand, my Dad thought it was great. "Now you don't have to buy that damned trailer", he proclaimed. He never called it a mobile home. It was always a trailer to him.

He finished up by asking, "Why don't you go and get a decent place to live?"

Embarrassing!

So there you have it. My first attempt at purchasing a home – I use the term "home" loosely – ended in failure. I got shot down for an $11,000 loan on a mobile home.

How embarrassing!

Well, you've got to start somewhere and I suppose this was my start. I was out of the race before the gun even went off.

But, at least I got up to the starting line.

I've learned over the years, never belittle humble beginnings. Remember, mighty oak trees were once little seedlings.

Dave Ives

Started renting in Huber Heights

Now, I switched my focus to finding a place to rent.

I got in the car and headed straight for the Air Force Base bedroom community of Huber Heights. I liked the town immediately. Good affordable housing with great proximity to the base. Mr. Huber knew what he was doing when he built this town.

We visited the Huber Real Estate rental office and landed a very nice two bedroom townhouse for $550 a month. They had a deal where if you paid on or before the first of the month, you could knock off a sizeable portion of the rent. I can't quite remember how much but I believe the discount was on the order of $50!

What a great concept. If you've ever been on the collecting side of rent you can see how this plan would be brilliant, keeps your cash flow coming with minimal hassle. The tenant has a tremendous incentive to pay on time.

Have you ever tried to collect overdue rent? Not fun …

We always paid on or before the 1st of the month. And, I was happy to do it. I loved getting the rent discount!

We were good tenants. What a great claim to fame. "Hey grandson, did you know your grandparents were good tenants. We always paid our rent on time. And our landlord became very wealthy."

Now that's something to brag about ...?

Coming to terms with some financial facts of life

It was difficult for me to come to terms with some hard facts.

First, I had a hard time understanding why my pay didn't go up as fast as the cost of living, especially housing. I remember an agent taking me to see an old standard run-of-the-mill home in Dayton priced at $105,000. I couldn't believe you had to pay that much money for a "nothing special" home in Dayton. I remember thinking this seemed like a big jump in ordinary home prices from four years ago when I lived in Columbus, Ohio and visited Dayton often. Mentally, I was still living in the past, thinking house prices would stay constant so my pay could eventually catch up! Well, it appeared that house prices jumped $20,000 or more in the time I was away. But, my pay only jumped about $15,000. I was not keeping up.

This was hard for me to accept. Somehow, I figured my pay would go up and house prices would stay the same.

I had a lot to learn about finances. I was enrolled in the Real World, On-the-Job, Hard Knocks, Trial and Error School of Finance (RWOJHKTESF - the military would love a nice big juicy acronym like this!) And, to this day I'm still attending. I'll never graduate, always learning.

My formal financial education was severely limited. I remember one high school teacher showing us how to balance a checkbook. And, I remember taking classes in micro and macroeconomics in college. I remember taking the classes, I don't remember anything else! That's the extent of my formal financial education!

Next, I had a difficult time ignoring the inputs of people who also didn't have a financial education, for instance – my Dad. I loved him, but I shouldn't have been looking to him for financial advice.

Now you may say that's a bit harsh, but is it?

My Dad had virtually no experience in mountain climbing. Would I ask him for advice on how to climb Mt Everest? Would my father be upset if I didn't ask him for mountain climbing advice? Would he be upset if he found out I sought the advice a mountain climbing expert instead?

– Probably not.

Why doesn't the same logic apply to financial advice? My Dad struggled with finances. He seemed to worry about money a lot. He seemed uncomfortable with money. He never seemed to have enough. It didn't look to me like he was moving ahead financially. Why then would I listen to his advice when it came to finances?

But, that's what I did.

When my Dad laughed at my idea to buy the mobile home, I was shocked. I thought it was a great idea. It had a lot of merits. I thought he would have congratulated me on my astute financial plan of attack. But, he didn't. And when I heard his reaction, I felt rejected. I took it personally. My Dad was laughing at another one of my stupid ideas. And, here's where I fell down, I listened and believed him. He was my Dad. He always knew what to do. He's more experienced. I'd better listen to him or I'll make a big mistake and hear those dreaded words, "I told you so."

Now I know better. This is wrong thinking on my part. I should have dismissed my Dad's input and moved on with my plan. It's called "doing your own thinking." I was still in the mode of letting others do the thinking for me. I didn't want to look stupid nor have people laugh at me, especially my father.

But, I've learned over the years you don't take advice from people who don't know, who don't have the experience, who have never done it. And, if people want to laugh – regardless of who they are – let them.

The mobile home deal

Now, let's look a little closer at my goofy mobile home deal.

I was going to buy a mobile home for $11,000. The Air Force was going to pay me a housing allowance of $500 per month, plus another $100 known as a variable housing allowance. Both of these incomes are tax free, a very nice benefit for military members. The lot fee was going to run about $100 per month which included utilities.

My father had never seen the mobile home so how could he correctly judge the situation. It was quite comfortable and the trailer park was located on base, therefore close to work and shops. It was a very livable environment. Not a place to brag to your friends about, but probably not a bad place to live either, especially if you're just starting and looking to move ahead financially. It's called making sacrifices. And, it's also called "not trying to keep up with the Joneses," a foreign concept for a lot of people.

So, to me it looked like a no-brainer, "Let me get this straight ... I can buy this home for $11,000. I have the funds to pay it off in about six months or less. I've got the cash in the bank. I can pocket virtually all my tax free housing allowance every month!"

Oh, by the way, there was no property tax on the home because it was located on the Air Force Base - federal land, another nice perk.

So, from my limited financial background perspective, this is how I saw the deal:

I pay $11,000 and get a place to live. I own it.

I have the money so I can pay off any loan virtually straight away leaving no debt.

This $11,000 investment will allow me to pocket about $400 to $500 a month in tax free military housing allowance! That's a crazy return on investment – well over 40%! If I live in base housing, the Air Force will take away my housing allowance. If I rent a place somewhere downtown, it will take up virtually all of my housing allowance.

I loved the idea of having extra cash each month and not struggling financially.

WORKING MY "BUT" OFF!

I figured once we started saving some serious cash, we could begin hunting for a "normal" home; look for bargains; find a good deal.

At this time I didn't know about the veteran's administration (VA) loans where they'd lend me money with nothing down. Also, I was experiencing housing "sticker shock" and I didn't want to pay $80,000 to $100,000 for a home. To me, an $11,000 price tag – and positive tax free housing allowance cash flow – looked better ... a lot better.

Was the $11,000 a fair price for the mobile home?

I don't know. I didn't get that far into the negotiations. Had my loan application been approved, I would have started looking at the mobile home with a bigger magnifying glass. I would have started shopping around. Looking to see if this represented a good buy.

But, even if I was able to shave a couple of thousand bucks off the price, it didn't really matter to me. The deal just seemed like an all-around winner, even at the asking price!

Now, the mobile home would probably not appreciate in value so later on I may not be able to get my $11,000 back. But, there's a more creative solution – I could rent it out to another family. I don't think it would have been too difficult to find a tenant at just $100 per month, representing a nice solid 11% return. It would probably rent for more. If the base wouldn't allow me to rent it out, then I'd just move it to another trailer park and put up the "for rent" sign – no problem. This could have been my first rental property, creating a nice little passive income stream.

Passive income is my favorite income.

Yes, it seems to me, buying the mobile home would have been a great way to get started in property investment and would have accelerated the process. But, instead I had to have a "normal" home and pay "normal" rent. The problem with "normal" is you end up like all the other "normal" people - the masses - who struggle financially.

Keep moving!

I got shot down for a loan, even though I shouldn't have been shot down.

SO WHAT?

DOESN'T MATTER!

I should have kept moving, kept pursuing the goal, kept attacking. For instance, why didn't I negotiate a cash price with the seller? Then offer to pay $5,000 up front and then the rest in installments over six months? Or, come up with some other arrangement to make the deal happen?

Instead I regrouped and consolidated. Fell back into my secure financial comfort zone and spent the next six months or so fixing my credit report issue.

Getting turned down for a loan doesn't have to stop you from achieving your property investing goals. Yes, it slowed me down - it took my focus away for a while - but it didn't stop me.

WORKING MY "BUT" OFF!

Don't waste time worrying about the loan you didn't get. Instead, focus on getting the loan – getting the deal, and stay focused until you get it! You may have to talk to a lot of people, a lot of banks, and a lot of lenders. You may have to work a side deal with the seller. You may have to do a lot of research, legwork and red-tape untangling. You may have to do some fancy footwork, some dancing, and even a bit of jumping through hoops before you finally hear the magic word - APPROVED!

9 BUT, HOW DO I GET MY FIRST RENTAL PROPERTY?

Not sure the best way to get your first rental property ... but here's why and how I did it.

Wanting to Buy

It's early 1993 and I'm a newly commissioned civilian. Still working at the base (Wright-Patterson) as an engineer in virtually the same position I had while in the Air Force. I want to buy a house. But, housing prices seem high in Dayton, Ohio. We start to look at alternatives. We get a little creative. In the end, we get our first house but it's not in Dayton ...

Rents keep going up!

"Rents always go up – we should buy." I told myself as I sipped my coffee at the table in my rented condo.

I never felt comfortable with renting. Every year you can look forward to the stress of having to deal with a rent increase. Even if the rent doesn't go up, you still get to deal with the stress of worrying about it! So, as with most things that bother me, I decided to develop a plan to deal with it. My plan was to look at buying a house.

House for retirement

Part of my motivation was to have a home in retirement. I wanted to make sure we had a decent house to live in during our later years. It seemed to me, if we bought it now, it should be paid off by the time we retire, one less thing to stress about in retirement. Now, if we had plenty of money in retirement we could always buy another house. But I just wanted something that would be there for us in case we didn't have the money. I guess my thinking was a bit draconian and leaning way over to the conservative side, but I wanted to hedge my bets and make sure we were covered.

Learning from the old timers

Part of this overly conservative thinking came from my observations of the guys retiring from work. A lot of them seemed to be overly stressed about their retirement, stressed about finances. And, one subject that seemed to pop up fairly often was housing. They expressed concerns about being able to pay for their retirement homes on their pension. They expressed concerns about high housing costs. At least compared to what the costs were years ago when they first started their careers.

I listened and learned.

Ken's story

Let me share one story with you that really stands out in my memory. It's a conversation with my office mate Ken. He'd been working at the base for well over 20 years after spending four years as an Air Fo;rce officer. Let me tell you a little about Ken before I jump into our conversation.

Ken was a big guy. Not tall but very wide. He seemed to sit at his desk from the time he came to work until he went home. I can't remember him getting up during the day. Of course he must have, but I just don't remember it. He seemed to always be at his desk.

He smoked a lot. Now you may wonder, how did he smoke a lot if he hardly ever got up from his desk? Easy, he just lit up at his desk. There was a no smoking policy but Ken lit up anyway and the management didn't have the nerve to tell him to stop.

Apparently, in the old days people smoked at their desks. No drama. It was the norm, the "done" thing. Ken was from the old days. He'd been smoking at his desk for years. He wasn't about to stop just because some new policy went into effect. Ken and management had an unwritten agreement; he could smoke at his desk. No one mentioned Ken's smoking as long as it was confined to his desk and his office area. And, as long as none of the other office workers complained, he was free to smoke. Essentially he was "grandfathered." The no-smoking policy didn't apply to him.

WORKING MY "BUT" OFF!

There was another old timer in the office and he didn't mind Ken's smoking. As for me, I moved into the office knowing full well that Ken smoked so I wasn't really in a position to complain. I felt Ken's smoking situation was not nearly as bad as the toxic "personality" situation I'd dealt with in my previous office. So I moved into Ken's office. And, my desk was next to the window so I really didn't mind his smoking too much.

Ken was a cheerful, productive and smart fellow but very set in his ways. He typed away at the computer all day working on his C++ programs. He seemed to enjoy his work as long as management left him alone.

Ken was not a meetings guy. On rare occasions he would be cajoled into going to some mandatory meeting but it was never an easy task for management.

He was a guy who produced results. He wrote programs that worked. He was the "go-to" guy on the floor. If someone needed a program to calculate fuel flow for a new ramjet engine design, they'd see Ken. If someone had a question about rocket trajectory analysis, they'd see Ken.

And, he was personable. He got along well with just about everyone. He was from the south, Pell City Alabama to be exact. He had a nice southern drawl. I liked him.

"Well, Dave, let me tell ya." Ken liked to start with a down home friendly lead in, very good conversational style. Let's the listener get adjusted before starting in with any heavy details.

Dave Ives

"I remember when we first came to Ohio (pronounced Uh-hi-a) and we bought our first house. Nine thousand bucks for a three bedroom house near the base. My hand was shaking as I signed the paperwork. Dang, that was almost as much money as I made in a year! I couldn't get over paying that much money for a house. But, my wife wanted it, so we got it." Ken explained.

I'd been talking about buying a house and had been complaining about how the prices seemed so high. Ken was now giving me some background on the housing situation in Dayton over the years.

Ken continued his story. "Then after a few years my wife started talking to the other wives about the houses up in Huber Heights. They were more modern, had bigger rooms, fancy kitchens and bathrooms. And they had attached garages. They were top of the line. And, guess what?"

I just stared back at Ken waiting for the answer to his rhetorical question.

"My wife had to have one too!" He answered his own question.

"So, a few months later, I'm settin at a big fancy desk in some bank filling out more paperwork. You should have seen me shaking this time. Not just my hand, but my whole body, just a shaking. The house was costin me about $14,000! That was more than I made in a whole year workin. I couldn't believe we were gonna pay that much money for a house!" Ken said with a tone of excitement way outside his normal even keel level.

"There you have it Dave. I couldn't believe paying that much money for a house back then and now it seems like nothing. The same house today is fetchin maybe $80,000. I don't know how people do it these days. They're making $40 grand a year and buying a house that cost them twice that. And, they think nothing of signing the paperwork. No shaking, no sweating. Just sign away. Don't know how they do it."

I listened. What he said stuck with me. I was one of those folks, people looking at paying over twice their annual salary to buy a house!

"Wouldn't it be great to just pay about forty grand for a nice house? That would only be one year's pay. What a deal that would be." I thought.

But no, times had changed. A nice house now costs eighty thousand – twice as much. All I kept wondering was how much would houses cost in another ten years? Would they be twice as much again? Even if they only went up 25%, the price tag would hit one hundred thousand. Is my pay going to go up that much in ten years? Don't think so, especially, if I keep working as an engineer. I see what the other engineers are making – guys who are ten years further down the track – and it's not exciting. I see what kind of cars they drive, where they live, how they pinch pennies, definitely not exciting.

Ken's story had a big influence on me. It convinced me to take action. It convinced me to buy a house now. Not in a few years, not after the kids get older, not when I think I have enough money, but now. Right now!

Look for a house

So, my wife Marieta and I started looking.

We began our search in the Dayton area. I remember looking at older homes near the base, nothing too fancy, no extras; very old homes. And, I remember the prices, about $105,000. I felt very uncomfortable with this number. It just didn't make sense to me – price too high, income too low.

But, I still had a burning desire to buy now.

So, how to solve this dilemma? Yes, I wanted to buy now, but the numbers didn't make sense financially. I didn't want to spend that much money especially when I saw the houses. Seemed like a lot of money for not much house. And, I felt my income was way too low to justify spending around the $100,000 mark.

I started thinking and thinking. I want a house for when we retire. That's the driving motivation here. So what other options can we explore?

Then an idea shot into my head, "I wonder how much it would cost to build a brand new home on our land in Florida?" We had an acre of land just sitting there doing nothing, what if we could put it to use? What if the numbers made more sense?

Remember, this is the one acre block of land I bought on my accidental trip to Florida with my mom and dad. To read about the whole ridiculous episode see the previous chapter, "But, How do I get started?"

I made a phone call to a realtor in Florida and asked about house prices.

"We can build you a beautiful, brand new three bedroom home on your land for seventy thousand," Dottie said with complete assurance. "We have our own builder who'll give you a ten year guarantee. It's a very simple process."

Off to Florida ...

Marieta and I booked a short holiday to Florida to find out more.

We arrived in beautiful Tampa Florida and drove up highway 75 to Citrus County. Then we started looking.

Dottie took us through the display home, beautiful, with three bedrooms and a two car garage on a huge lot. Nice lanai in the back, brand new carpet, large bedrooms, great big master bedroom with walk-in closet leading to the big spacious master bathroom. The other two bedrooms and the family bathroom were all spacious and very well presented. As you walk into the home you're hit with the big great living room which opens to the dining room and off to the left you see the long kitchen counter - very impressive. Nice big open plan arrangement.

I looked over at Dottie and asked, "So, you mean to tell me you can build this same house on our one acre lot for seventy grand?"

"Yup. That's right. What are you waiting for?" Dottie replied almost before I finished my question.

I'm not sure of my exact words but I think I said something amazingly original like, "Where do I sign?"

But, we didn't sign right then and there. Instead Marieta and I went back to our hotel to discuss our options. We could pay about $100,000 in Dayton and get an old house without a lot of the trimmings or we could build a brand new home on our one acre lot for $70,000.

Then I asked Marieta the magic question, "Where would you rather retire, Dayton or Florida?"

I called up Dotty the next day and told her, "We'll take one just like the model home you showed us yesterday."

Before you could say "mortgage" we were in the sales office meeting with a slew of people ready to sell us their wares.

First on the scene was the lady from the bank.

"No problem. We'll get you a loan. Use your land as collateral so you don't have to put anything down. Do you want a fixed or variable rate loan?"

I responded like the seasoned professional I was, "Huh?"

She explained the loan options and we finally went with a variable even though I felt slightly uncomfortable about it. But, she was convincing and I was unknowing, so that's what we ended up with.

Next, we visited with the curtains person.

Marieta took over here. It was all a blur to me. I couldn't care less. Just get something that won't offend renters.

Then we discussed tiles. You'll have to wait until Marieta writes her book to find out where this conversation went. I had the same attitude as before; just pick something that won't repulse renters. Something neutral that doesn't evoke hostile reactions.

The parade of salespeople seemed to go on forever and I got more and more bored. But, the procession finally ended and we were dismissed for the day. We then got on a plane and headed back to Dayton. We would have to wait several months to see our new home.

Building process ...

I remember the building process went rather well. At least it seemed so from 1000 miles away. After all, we were in Ohio, the house in Florida.

The builder kept us informed of progress. They sent plans. They called with any questions about our preferences. They were like a good waiter, talked to us just enough to let us enjoy the process and look after our needs but not so much as to be a bother. My attitude was really one of "hands off." Just build the house and call me when it's done.

I learned later on that not everybody took this approach. I remember a person who worked with me at the labs (Wright-

Patterson Air Force Base) who'd come into work every day detailing the dramas with building his home.

From the way he was talking, the builder had virtually no freedom from supervision. It seemed the builder had to get approval from this guy before hammering in each nail! He seemed like he was taking "pedantic" to a new level. I wonder how anyone could work in such a micromanagement environment.

I also wonder how the house came out. I wonder if the builder just walked away half way through. I wonder if the builder didn't just end up decking the guy.

I personally wouldn't want to have someone looking over my shoulder – critiquing my every move – while I'm working. Would you?

Would you want your builder to dislike you immensely? Or, might it be better to have a good working relationship with your builder?

If the builder is not doing his job, then you fire him. That's different. But, if the builder is good, then I'd prefer to tell him what I want done and then let him do it.

It was a bit hard for me to micromanage our building process given the separation between me and the building site. And, I suppose that was ok. I had no intention of micromanaging the project anyway.

Then one day the phone rang. "The house is done. When can you come down for the closing?" Dottie asked excitedly. She was looking forward to payday. Closing day is the day she gets paid her commission.

Back down to Florida ...

We booked another trip to Florida.

The house came out great. Just like the model we saw those months earlier. Except our house was reversed; garage on the other side. This was one of the changes the builder recommended based on the slope of our land. We agreed and the builder pressed two or three keys on the computer and the plans were redrawn to reflect the change.

The only sore spot was the landscaping. I'd call it "modern sand trap." Great for working on your sand wedge swing but not very attractive around a new home.

We did have some grass put in the front yard and a bit on the sides but the back yard was all sand. From the road you could see the sand in the back and the front where the grass ended. We probably needed about twice the amount of grass to get a good look.

Marieta and I ended up going to the hardware store and picking up grass seed and other items to carry out lawn care. I remember racking, shoveling and spreading grass seed. I'm not sure our efforts gave us any lasting benefit, but at least we got in there and made an attempt. Looking back on it I wish we had just ordered more sod (grass) and had it installed. But, the extra sod wasn't cheap and we were probably looking to save a few bucks.

We visited the bank where they plopped a mountain of paperwork in front of us. I remember reading pages saying something like, "Don't sign unless you understand what it means!" I made a futile attempt to read seemingly endless pages of fine print but gave up after about five minutes. It was double talk, pure gobbledygook.

I quickly realized if we didn't sign, we didn't get the house. So, Marieta and I started signing every page they put in front of us. When it was over, we both came down with a bad case of writer's cramp.

Then we visited the local property management business and signed an agreement. I think we had it rented before we left. The rent was $650 per month, which pretty much covered all our expenses.

Retirement home- rental property

Technically, I acquired my first rental property as a by-product of wanting a home in retirement. Not a very direct strategy for starting a property investment portfolio, but a start none the less.

Essentially, I stumbled into my first rental property. If prices were lower in Dayton, we probably would have bought a home and lived in it. This would have delayed our rental property start.

So, how do you get your first rental property?

WORKING MY "BUT" OFF!

Again, I'm not sure of the best way. I can only share with you how I did it. And, hopefully my sharing will inspire you. Let you know it can be done. It's not complicated. You can do it too.

I would even suggest that it may be better to buy a rental property first, before you buy a home to live in. You see a positive cash flow rental property gets you in the game, puts you in business. It sets you up to make additional income.

Are you OK with additional income?

10 BUT, HOW DO I KNOW IF IT'S A GOOD BUY?

I overcame this BUT in a rather boring and conventional way – I rolled up my sleeves, put on my work boots and then went out and did a bit of basic research along with some good old fashioned legwork!

Now, when I say research, I don't mean taking out a local government grant and burning through thousands of taxpayer dollars on useless mind numbingly complicated analysis!

No!

I'm talking about common sense research. The same kind you do virtually every day to determine what is, and what isn't, a good buy.

For instance, how do you determine if you're getting a good buy on a bicycle? If you go down to the bike store every Saturday for six months and see your dream bicycle priced at $369, then when you

WORKING MY "BUT" OFF!

walk in the next Saturday and see a big discount tag with a new price - $269 – you might figure it's a good buy! And, if you checked on-online and other stores to discover the $369 is the going price, then you're extremely confidant the new $269 price is a great buy.

It's the same quality bike. The bike hasn't changed; only the price - 27% lower. Therefore, by anyone's accounting, this appears to be a good buy.

Why wouldn't this same basic research apply to buying property?

It would.

And, this is what I found out back in 1994 while looking for a home. I was sick and tired of renting and decided to start looking around for a house to buy. What I discovered amazed me. I could buy a quality home for less than its market value, a savings of $10,000 or more, nearly a 13% discount. By anyone's accounting, a good deal.

My regret was not discovering this earlier. It turns out, the deal had been on the table all along, offered by the same company I rented my home from. I just wasn't aware of it.

And, there is the biggest problem facing most of us. A very subtle problem that's easy to overlook, easy to miss.

You see, prior to my house hunting expedition – I wasn't looking! I had my eyes and ears closed to any deals involving property! My house hunting – deal finding – antenna was down, turned off, not receiving any signals!

How can you find something when you're not looking for it? How can you find a good buy on a home when you're not even looking? And, if you happened to come across a good deal how would you even know it?

And, therein lies a second major problem facing most people – including me. They wouldn't know a good deal if it came up and bit them in the face!

How can you know if it's a good deal – a good buy – if you haven't got any idea of value, of pricing?

I find myself in this situation when I shop at the grocery store. I hardly ever shop at the grocery store but on the rare occasion when I do, I'm lost when it comes to value and pricing. I just put the items on the checkout counter and pay whatever rings up on the register. I'm not familiar with grocery store prices and therefore susceptible to overpaying, getting ripped off.

And, I'm OK with that. I would rather understand property prices and values, concentrate on getting good buys on investment properties. That way I can pay for my expensive groceries!

By the way, I have a safeguard in place for my lack of grocery buying prowess. You see, my wife, Marieta, is a grocery shopping expert. She's so good at getting bargains, I feel it's only fair I shop sometimes and overpay. Let the store recoup some of their losses!

Tired of Renting

It was early 1994 and we already had a rental property in Florida. Now, I was looking to buy a home for us to live in. I was tired of paying dead rent money, tired of the annual rent rise ritual, tired of helping the landlord get wealthy.

We were living in Huber Heights, Ohio, just north of Dayton. I was working at Wright-Patterson, Air Force Base in the aero-propulsion laboratory as an engineer.

Even though I had very little experience in property, I was able to discover a good buy. And, the main reasons for my discovery are very simple. First, I was looking. You're chances of making a gainful discovery go up – way up – if you're looking! Next, I luckily talked to the right people. These "right people" were right in front of me the whole time - I just didn't know it. I happened to call and ask them questions. No one told me to call them. No one recommended I call them. I just decided to call as part of my search, part of my campaign to buy a home, part of my determination to get a good buy.

So, here's the story – one example - about how I stumbled across finding a good buy.

Dave Ives

A good buy or a goodbye?

What a deal!

"Hey, honey, I notice the townhouse down the street is for sale. I think I'll go check it out." I told my wife Marieta. I made the short walk and did a curbside visual inspection, same as our house. No surprise. Every townhouse in the neighborhood was essentially the same. Ok, maybe different color paint, maybe the garage was on the opposite side, maybe a slightly larger yard, but the reality ... they were all the same! Nice, two bedroom townhouses with attached two car garages on small blocks of land.

But, what did surprise me is the discovery that some folks were owners. I thought everybody rented like us.

I was intrigued by this townhouse for sale. One of my neighbors was in a position to make a bit of cash. This opened up my eyes to a fairly basic reality – when you own, you have a chance of making some money. But, when you rent, there's virtually no chance, in the end, all I'd have left is a pile of crumpled rent receipts!

Then I called the realtor and found out the asking price, $55,000. My brain went into overdrive. "Hey, I can afford that! We could own our own place instead of renting. Wow!" I was excited.

I had no idea if that was a good price or not. No idea if it represented good value. I was excited because it was less than what I expected and I felt confident I could qualify for that loan amount.

WORKING MY "BUT" OFF!

Then out of nowhere I had a crazy idea. What if I call my rental company and ask about buying the place we're living in now? I figured if we could get it for $55,000 why not just stay here?

We were renting from the Huber Home Rentals. Why not at least explore this option, why not try, see if there's any possibility of them selling? I didn't really believe anything would come of it but for some reason I picked up the phone and dialed.

"Hello, this is Huber Sales may I help you?" came the pleasant voice over the phone.

"Yes, this is Dave Ives and I'm wondering if you folks would consider selling the property we're currently renting from you?"

I could hardly believe my ears when the lady responded as follows:

"We sell our rentals all the time. When a tenant leaves, the home goes to both the sales and rental departments. Then it's just a matter of who's first. If the sales team finds a buyer, it's sold. If the rental team finds a tenant then we rent it out. It doesn't really matter to us either way."

And the best part – the price.

"You're in the first house on Marti Gras right?" She asked and then proceeded.

"We'll sell it to you for $45,000. That's below market. We do that because we want the houses to sell quickly. Mr. Huber doesn't want them sitting around. It's the same reason we give big rent discounts, Mr. Huber wants them rented or sold – fast!"

I almost jumped through the phone! My only question, "How soon can we do the deal?"

Remember, the advertised property down the street was on the market for $55,000. So, when the Huber representative told me I could have my place for $45,000, I felt it was a bargain, below market value, just as she claimed. This Huber pricing represented an 18% discount over the same property down the street!

If I didn't make that call, I wouldn't have known this deal even existed! Huber didn't advertise. It appeared they relied on word of mouth. Maybe, they had a list of potential buyers a mile long and therefore never needed to advertise.

How many deals like this are happening in your neighborhood and you don't even know about it? Maybe it's time to make some phone calls!

Shot Down!

Well, I wish I could tell you I bought the home but I can't. I got shot down, not by Mr. Huber but by Mr. Finance. I wanted to use my Veteran's Administration (VA) benefits but couldn't because the home didn't fall into one of their approved categories. As a townhouse in a neighborhood with mostly rentals, the VA wouldn't go for it. I was too unfamiliar with finance and didn't know where to turn so I dropped it.

Looking back I wish I had pursued the finance with more vigor. I'm sure I could have worked some kind of deal had I been more persistent. Maybe look at alternate methods, buy directly from Mr. Huber under owner finance or some other creative arrangement. I just don't know because I didn't ask, I didn't investigate, I didn't go any further.

I let this good deal get away from me.

But, I learned a valuable lesson ... I learned how to find a good property deal. I learned that I could do it. I learned that I could do it on my own. I learned that it's relatively easy, no special skills, no special education required.

For some reason, I didn't think to ask Huber about other homes for sale. I wish I could go back in time to uncover my exact thinking, because it doesn't make sense to me know. It doesn't make sense that I would uncover this "discount" market and then not aggressively go after it.

But, that's what I did ... I stopped the hunt, at least for a while.

Later that year ...

I was talking to a co-worker who told me about the great deal he got on a house in Huber Heights. This prompted me to go looking again.

"Yeah, we just got a great deal on our house up in Huber." Bob stated with a bit of excitement and pride in his voice during our little hallway chat.

"What do you mean by a great deal?" I questioned.

"Well, we got it for over $10,000 less than its value. That's their sales strategy, they just put the price well below what other similar properties are selling for and they sell them quickly." Bob explained.

By this point my jaw was on the ground. I wanted some of this action. How do I get a deal like this? I made up my mind to give the Huber Sales office another call.

"Hello, I'm calling to find out if you have any properties for sale?" I asked trying to sound as if I do this all the time.

"What price range are you interested in?" came the lady's response in a very measured and assured tone.

"Have you got anything in the 60 to 70 thousand range?" I replied and then waited for the laughter on the other end of the line. Nicer, three bedroom, stand-alone houses in Huber Heights were selling for about $80,000 and above.

"We get them all the time. Would you like me to give you a call if one comes up?"

A bit flustered, excited and surprised, I managed a half composed reply, "Sure."

Several days later the phone rang. It was the lady from the Huber Sales office.

WORKING MY "BUT" OFF!

"Hello Dave. I've got two properties for you to look at in your price range. They're just down the street from each other. I'll give you the addresses and you and your wife can go by and have a look. Just stop by the office and I'll give you the keys."

This was a very interesting phone call. Let me get this straight, I stop by the sales office, pick up the keys and then go show myself the houses? I thought she would offer to pick me up, then drive us to the properties, and then give us a personal walk through and then ... But, no ... "If you want to look at them come by and get the keys."

Marieta and I stopped by the office to pick up the keys. We then made the short drive to the first home and had a walk through. It looked great, a simple straight-forward property. Three bedrooms, nice kitchen, open living area, attached one car garage, large flat lot with nice looking homes on all sides. I got excited as I kept thinking, "If I could get this place for $70,000 that would be a great buy."

We then drove down to the street to the other property. A very short drive, only four or five houses away. I liked this one better because it had a two car garage. But, the house layout was not as favorable and it was a bit smaller than the other one.

I remember feeling like a little kid running up and down the street between the two houses trying to decide which one to get. In my mind I half wondered what the neighbors were thinking as they watched me skip back and forth poking my nose into the two vacant houses. Also, I remember discounting these thoughts because, essentially, I didn't care. For me, this was the deal of the century, I was pumped!

You mean to tell me I can have either one of these houses for the ridiculously low price of $70,000? That's the question that ran through my mind as my body ran between the two houses.

My thoughts raced ... $70,000 that's it? Wow, why isn't there a line-up to buy these houses? Where are all the people hiding? Surely, they must know this is a great deal?

I knew if we bought either one of these houses for $70,000, we could turn around and sell it the next day for $80,000. The little bit of research I'd done and the experience I had dealing with the Huber reduced sales (even though I never bought), told me this was a no-brainer.

Also, there was a house for sale across the street - same model as the first house we looked at - on the market for $83,000. It sold in a relatively short time.

We knew our home was worth at least $80,000 the day we bought it.

Marieta and I drove back to the Huber sales office and delivered our verdict; - we'll take the first house, 8361 Schoolgate Drive. It was Marieta's choice. And, I admit, it was the better of the two homes. I just had a bit of a challenge giving up the two car garage!

I still get excited when I think about that purchase. It was like buying a pair of shoes. Try on a few pairs and then pick the one you like best! It was one of the most pleasant real estate buying experiences I've had. It made planning for a holiday look like hard work. It was – dare I say – fun!

I used my VA loan benefit to purchase the home with no money down. The VA had no issues lending against this solid stand-alone home in a great neighborhood. We signed the mountain of paperwork and were the proud owners of our first primary residence home.

Up to this point we'd always rented.

We were entering a new era.

A good buy or a goodbye?

How did I know this was a good buy?

My "good buy" decision was again reinforced when a few months later I visited my neighbor down the street. They had just bought their home and invited us over for a look.

"We paid $110,000!" said the wife in an excited voice without any prompting.

I then asked, "Who was the selling agent?"

She mentioned some local real estate company.

That's all I needed to hear. Yes, the house was a little bigger than ours. It had a two car garage instead of our one car garage. But, other than that, it was the same house, same Huber home look; same general feel.

So, my neighbors paid $40,000 more for their home. As I looked around, I couldn't see the extra value. Maybe $10,000, or maximum $20,000, but not $40,000 – no way.

As I viewed their home I asked myself, "Would I be $40,000 happier living here?"

Apparently, these folks didn't talk to Mr. Huber. They didn't know about the unadvertised deals. I didn't mention anything as they'd already bought the home. No sense telling them now.

Why did you sell?

Our new home was a gem from day one.

I wish I could tell you we still have it and it's making lots of money for us. But, sadly, I can't.

This property is another case of a lesson hard learned. One and a half years after the purchase, we sold the property and moved from Ohio.

The sales plan was simple, if it sells great, but if it doesn't we'll rent it out. We put the house on the market for $81,000 and it sold before the agent put up the sign in the front yard.

Big Mistake!

Oops! Several mistakes here ...

WORKING MY "BUT" OFF!

First, we let the realtor talk us into setting a low price. His rationale – it'll sell fast. And, boy was he right! He had the home sold the day after we signed the agent agreement. He even debated whether or not to put up the "For Sale" sign. What for? The house was virtually sold! But, I do recall the sign going up even though it was meaningless. The deal went through without a hitch.

I suppose the rationale for the sign was to attract backup buyers in case our primary buyer backed out. And, boy did we attract buyers. They were waiting like hungry sharks ready to strike. If the primary buyer hesitated, we had plenty of people circling the deal ready to sink their teeth into a great buying opportunity!

We bought it for $70,000 and sold it a year and a half later for $81,000. Not bad. But, I still feel it was a mistake to sell.

Our plan was to rent it out if it didn't sell. Doesn't that suggest we should have set a higher asking price? If we don't get the handsome price, then we just put it on the rental market, no problem - so what if it doesn't sell?

And – as I ask myself to this day – why did we sell? Why didn't we just keep it? The house was a dream rental. Let's go over why.

First, it had everything most people would want in a home – attached garage, large kitchen with all the associated appliances. Also, it had a large master bedroom and bath, two large bedrooms and a family bathroom. A spacious back yard completed the package.

To add value, we made improvements along the way. First, we replaced the old clunky manual garage door with a brand new white automatic one. We also added a matching front security door. We were amazed how these two simple features made the house stand out in a beautiful way.

The automatic garage door was Marieta's favorite, especially on freezing cold days when she returned home from grocery shopping.

Then we had the house painted. A relatively minor job since it was a brick house. The painting task consisted of the facing eve over the garage, the two eves at the end of the house and the trim areas including around the windows.

I remember getting the quote from a very young man (maybe 19 years old) and being a bit nervous about his price - $500. But, when he and his team were done, we had two coats of light blue paint to the main areas and two coats of white paint to the trim areas and best of all - the house looked awesome!

It's hard to believe what a good paint job can do to improve the looks of a home! I remember having a little spring in my step coming home to our beautiful house following the paint work. I also remember gladly writing the check and - with a big smile - handing it to the painter. I felt like we got excellent value for our money.

Other improvements included a white picket fence to separate the front and back lawn areas. The idea was to provide a back yard barrier for the children to play safely. We didn't want them straying out into the street.

Also, we had a nice colonial wooden shed built in the back yard to give us some storage space.

WORKING MY "BUT" OFF!

We installed a water softener. This was a very nice feature because prior to the install, you couldn't lather up in the shower no matter how much soap you piled on! The water was extremely hard. The water softener was a welcome creature comfort addition.

Of course, we always kept the yard neat and trim. Nothing fancy, just a simple clean cut appearance.

Taking all these improvements, the nice curb appeal and the extremely low price, it's no wonder the house sold to the first person who looked at it. They walked through the house before the realtor even put the sign in the front yard. Consequently, when the sign went up, the house was already sold.

Looking back on this, I wish we kept the property. As you can probably gather, it has a bit of sentimental value to me.

But, it also represents wealth. That house would probably pull in about $1,000 a month in rent today. My payments were only about $500 per month, expenses maybe another $300. How would you like an extra $200 or more coming in every month like clockwork over and above what you're already making? Do you know anyone who would say no to that proposition?

The Huber Heights area is the perfect rental spot for military personnel working at Wright-Patterson AFB. For a three bedroom, one car attached garage and all the nice features of this home, you would probably have an endless stream of customers lined up to rent your property.

Yes, I'm sentimental, but I'm also very keenly aware of how silly it was for us to sell that property. But, as my daughter tells me, "build a bridge Dad and get over it!"

I can do it and so can you!

Even though I made a mistake and sold the property, I still learned a very important and powerful lesson. I learned I can do basic research and determine a good buy. I can do it all by myself. I don't need a team of experts. I don't need a government agency to do it for me. I don't need a real estate agent to do it for me.

Yes, I can do it.

I can ask questions. I can talk to people. I can locate the people who make the sell decisions, the ones who know where the bargains are located.

I can follow obvious leads – why not first ask if I can buy the house I'm living in right now? Find out whom to call, and then pick up the phone and call them!

I learned that I don't have to wait around for permission, permission to hunt, permission to look, permission to find a good deal.

I can just get out there and do it.

And, you can too!

11 BUT, HOW DO I NEGOTIATE?

I got rid of this BUT by starting small. I learned some of my best negotiating lessons on small ticket items. The learning power in these low risk negotiating deals is immense.

Why?

Because, the lessons learned from small deals apply to big ticket items as well! The same principles translate up. If it works for buying a snow cone, it'll work for buying a ski resort! (Disclaimer: *I've never bought a snow cone or a ski resort!*)

So, if you want to learn how to negotiate buying a three bedroom home, you can start by negotiating a second hand dresser at a garage sale.

If you want to learn about negotiating from a seller's perspective, you can gain a lot of experience by opening a stall at your local weekend market.

Get your experience on low risk, low cost items and then apply this experience to big ticket items.

My most memorable negotiating lesson came while buying some second hand tools at a flea market. It cost me a few "pride" points, but the knowledge I gained from the lesson was priceless!

Flea Market Negotiating

It was early 1993. We were living in Dayton Ohio. I found myself strolling up and down the aisles at a local flea market. My wife, Marieta, loved going to these things and I was just tagging along as usual.

But, I'm glad I went because I learned an extremely valuable lesson. One that has stayed with me over the years and has probably made and saved me a lot of money. It's so simple, yet highly effective.

I took a little hit to my pride and my wallet that day, but the resulting lesson was worth it. The lesson came from a man selling tools. He simply brought to light my poor negotiating skills. I walked away from his table a bit dejected, but I should have been jumping up and down thanking him for his invaluable teaching lesson. Here's what happened.

A Lesson in Negotiation

"Wow! Look at these tools", I exclaimed. "I'll get this one. Oh yeah, I need a wrench too. These screwdrivers should come in handy." I was excited about getting my hands on some much needed tools and about getting them at a nice low price. Thank God for flea markets!

After gathering all my tools, I added up the total. Each item had been priced and the total cost came up to about $14.

I then thought for a moment, "Hmmm, since I'm buying in volume, why not ask for a discount?" So, I swaggered up to the merchant and as nonchalantly as I could, offered my proposal, "Would you take $12 for all these tools?"

Here's where the vendor gave me his lesson. He unabashedly pointed out my lack of negotiating skills. I was expecting him to haggle with me. But, he wouldn't hear of it. His response was outside my expectations.

He simply looked up at me from his comfortable seated position and stated – loudly enough so his buddies and anyone in proximity could hear – the words I've never forgotten,

"I would have taken less, but since you've offered $12, then $12 it is!"

Backfired

My heart sunk as I knew I was paying a higher price than necessary.

My ploy at negotiating had backfired and it was on display for all to see. The vendor and his buddies had a good laugh as they saw my jaw hanging and my lips quivering as I tried to think of something clever to say. But, nothing came out.

What was I going to say? "How, much less would you take?"

He'd just come back and say, "I'll take the $12 you offered thanks!"

My pride wouldn't let me walk away. Besides, I wanted the tools and I was getting them for less than the listed price, so it wasn't so bad.

I made an offer, he accepted, I paid him.

Inexpensive lesson

Although I didn't appreciate his style, I am forever grateful to this flea market vendor for the valuable lesson he taught me.

I didn't like his style because he could have let me think I made a smooth bargain. But, he chose to point out my blunder. Even though I felt I got a good buy, he told me the truth – he got the good deal. He got more money for the items than he would have otherwise accepted.

I'm grateful because this precious lesson only cost me about four or five bucks! But, it's worth millions.

WORKING MY "BUT" OFF!

What did I learn?

The lesson is very simple but very important – don't be the first to offer a price. Whenever possible and practical, have the other person offer a price first.

If I were in the flea market situation again, I would walk up and say something like, "Since I'm buying in volume (a little humor), would you offer a discount off the marked price?"

It really doesn't matter what answer comes back because my goal is to get a feel for the vendors lowest price.

If he says, "I'll knock a dollar off just for you." I could counter by saying, "I was looking for a much better deal. Tell you what, why don't I put them back and I'll look around some more and maybe come back later."

Usually, the vendor wants to cut the deal right then and there. They don't want to see if you'll come back later. Now, the ball's in the other guy's court. It wouldn't be unusual to hear a response along these lines, "You give me ten bucks now and they're yours."

What if you're the guy selling the tools? You're always at an advantage because you know your lowest price. The rule here is never go below your lowest price. Let the buyer walk if you can't get your lowest price or better.

But, the rule is the same. Let the buyer do the talking not you.

Think about it, you've already played your hand by setting the price on the item. Let the buyer do the talking to find out his highest price.

If I was selling at a flea market and a buyer approached with my "buying in volume discount" request, I might respond by saying, "What's it worth to you?"

I already know how low I can go. My job is to find the buyers highest price at or above my lowest selling price. If my customer is sharp I may hear something like, "It's not worth what you're asking, what's the lowest you'll go to get me to buy it right now?"

Ask questions

I must resist the urge to name a price. I know, it's hard, but I must do it or I'm taking the spice out of the exchange. A little discipline will take you a long way. I might reply by repeating the customer's question, "... Not worth the asking price? How do you figure?"

This forces the buyer to justify his/her statement and may lead to a settlement.

The buyer may be getting tired of the dialog and say, "I'll give you $12 for the lot."

Then I might think to myself, "I was willing to let it go for $10, so his offer is great." But, I wouldn't say it. Instead, I'd rub my chin and get fidgety and say something like, "Well, I normally don't like to give that big a discount but you are buying several items and I could use a sale right now so, I'll take it."

Now, everybody wins. The customer has negotiated a discount off the marked price and I've gotten a higher price than my minimum price. And, my customer leaves feeling he's cut a pretty nice bargain. Customers like to feel they've got a good bargain. I know I do.

Why such a big deal over a few tools?

You may be asking yourself right now, "Why is he making such a big deal about a nickel and dime exchange at a flea market?"

And, here's how I'd answer ...

Because the lesson is the same – and even more critical – for big ticket items!

I wouldn't want someone negotiating for me on a big ticket item who didn't understand this "don't offer a price first" concept. It could cost you thousands or even millions. A few well-placed words here and there and you could save yourself a bundle.

Don't ever underestimate the power of small learning opportunities. My real life flea market experience taught quicker and hit harder than any lesson I could learn from a book.

Head out to your nearest flea market!

So, I encourage you to go out soon to your nearest flea market, garage sale, whatever and get some experience negotiating. It'll be much more valuable than just reading it here.

12 BUT, WHAT IF I'M NO GOOD AT MAINTENANCE AND REPAIRS?

This is a BUT I overcame early in life.

I was about fifteen years old when I installed a concrete garage floor with my Dad. It was during this experience that I made an amazing discovery – you don't need to be good at maintenance and repairs! It's not a required skill. It's not needed.

Why?

Because there are "boatloads" of skilled people who are ready and eager to work for a reasonable price. You can hire the expertise you need.

Is it good to be knowledgeable in maintenance and repairs?

Yes! The more you know the better. It just means there are probably some tasks you can do yourself. Or, it means you have a better understanding of what needs to be done and can oversee work in a more competent manner. You'll probably make better decisions than someone who's less handy with the tools.

But, how many people are skilled in all areas of a particular industry? Isn't every industry specialized?

And that's why you get such fine craftsmanship. Folks are highly skilled in their specialized area of expertise.

Once you start to water down the trade, you see the workmanship fall off. The quality goes down. The finished product doesn't look as good, doesn't work as well and probably won't last as long.

For instance, would you hire a bricklayer to install your air-conditioning unit?

Yes, the bricklayer is an expert – an expert at laying bricks. But, does that skill transfer over to installing air conditioners?

And, the expert air conditioner installer probably lays a crooked row of bricks. Are you going to call him when you're looking for someone to build you a brick wall?

So, the question is this ... What kind of finished product do you want?

WORKING MY "BUT" OFF!

Do you want it to look good? Do you want it to look professional? Do you want it to last? Do you want it to hold up over time?

I'm guessing your answer is a resounding "YES" to all the above.

Also, when you go to sell or rent your home do you want folks to see quality or "good enough?" Do you want them to happily pay top dollar or find reasons to drive your asking price down?

People can sense quality. They can feel it a mile away.

They can also sense when someone has cut corners.

Most people prefer quality. And most seem willing to pay more to have it.

In the long run, quality always trumps "good enough."

And, that's the valuable lesson I learned a long time ago when helping my Dad put in our concrete garage floor. We had plenty of concrete, plenty of manpower but we were missing one key element, one key ingredient.

The lesson I learned that day has saved me lots of time, aggravation and money over the years. The lesson can be applied across many disciplines but it's especially useful when applied to building a property investment portfolio.

Here's the story ...

Dave Ives

The Garage Floor Project

"Everybody ready? Alright, let it fly!" My Dad gave the go ahead to let the truck driver pour his load of grey concrete sludge out onto the dirt.

This was no ordinary dirt. We worked hard getting it prepared for the moment the concrete truck would arrive and dump its load. We lovingly shoveled it evenly over the garage floor area. We used the level to make sure our floor would be straight. We packed it down to give our concrete a good resting place. We were proud of our sexy looking patch of dirt. We were ready for battle – bring on the wet concrete!

Our work crew consisted of me, my Dad, my brothers Steve and Paul, and another helper Tim. Tim was a hired hand, the son of Dad's friend Matt. Tim was two years older than my twin Steve and I and three years older than Paul. I was about fifteen. We were a willing band of workers, ready with our rakes, shovels and smoothing boards.

"Ok, boys, here she comes! Spread it around. Even it out!" barked my Dad as the concrete came flying down the chute. His confident commands made us feel proud to be part of the team. We were putting in a new garage concrete floor, an accomplishment we could brag about for years to come. It was going to be a dandy.

After about forty five minutes or so of working, my Dad's voice took on a more urgent and serious tone. "Now, move over here. Leave that alone and help over here - quick, before the stuff dries!"

WORKING MY "BUT" OFF!

I was just following instructions, not really worried about the overall picture. I could move concrete around like nobody's business, but the final touches would have to come from someone with concrete floor experience. I was ready and willing to follow instructions as they were commanded out.

The concrete was drying fast and the floor didn't look that good to me. I kept thinking, "What's the next step in the process? When do we get to the part where we make the floor look nice?"

I knew things were going bad. Dad's mood was taking a turn for the worse. His instructions were becoming less coherent as he blurted out, "God @#&*, this stuff is getting hard! Get over here! Move the – never mind – stay there and see if you can flatten it out!"

The crew scrambled – elbows flying, hips swinging, sweat dripping - but nothing was working. The floor was drying fast and our best efforts were not making any progress. It seemed the more we worked the concrete, the worse it got.

We were like a bad plastic surgeon, making you uglier and uglier with each operation.

Finally, we heard the command, the one we'd been expecting. Like the punch-drunk boxer wobbling on one knee waiting for the referee to call the fight, we knew the game was up. Although not a pleasant sound, the final bell came as a relief. It came when Dad said in a dejected voice, "Ok, boys, that's it. Leave it alone. We're done."

Dad put on a brave face as he thanked Tim. Then I saw the $10 bill exchange hands and thought, "That's a lot of money! Man, Tim made out pretty good today for a lousy two hours work."

My brother Steve and I worked at a nearby wild animal farm operating the rides and picking up trash. We pulled in about $1.63 an hour. I remember we'd get excited about breaking $60 take-home pay. To get the $60 net we had to work over 60 hours!

So, ten bucks was a lot of money! To me, it represented ten hours work!

Tim went home and Dad stood there staring at the freshly poured concrete floor. He was not in a good mood. As he scanned the bumpy and uneven floor, his mood sank further.

The reality didn't meet his expectation.

He expected a beautiful concrete floor. Like the ones you see at a brand new home, pristine bright concrete with professional looking grooves and an almost perfectly level surface.

We've all seen these great looking concrete floors. You can almost feel the aura given off by the amazing workmanship. You can sense it. The floor seems to possess a bold attitude. It almost says to you, "I'm good. I was built by a pro. Don't mess with me – I'm built to last."

It's the kind of floor that sells homes.

Our floor didn't talk big. It conveyed a much different attitude. If it could talk it would probably say something like, "Don't step on me. I'm ugly. I'm wrinkly and uneven. Nobody likes me."

Our team was willing. We were strong. We had a collective great attitude. But, we were missing one key ingredient. The same key ingredient that makes one business succeed where another fails, the same ingredient necessary for a successful climb up Mt Everest. The same ingredient needed to succeed in virtually any venture.

The missing ingredient was very simple and painfully obvious as the concrete grew harder and harder and became uglier and uglier.

Guessed it yet?

Here's the missing ingredient –

KNOW-HOW!

We needed a person on our team who knew how to put in a concrete floor!

I'll bet we could have hired an experienced concrete floor expert for maybe $50 or less. Ask him to come by for a couple of hours, bring tools and pay him $50 for his time. Or, pay him $100, doesn't matter. The money would be well spent.

Another way to get "know-how" is to acquire it. My Dad, my brothers and I could have spent a few months working on a concrete floor installation team. After gaining experience, we'd be in a much better position to go it alone.

The bottom line is this ... you've got to have someone on the team with the "know-how!" Without this person, the project is in big trouble. Without this person or persons, you're introducing big risk; you're setting yourself up for disappointment.

Have you ever visited someone's home and they bragged about their latest home improvement project? And, then they show you and you felt a bit embarrassed for them because it looks awful?

Then you hear the proud owner proclaim, "Would you believe, I did it myself?"

Your sense of politeness won't let you say what you're really thinking, "Yeah, I can tell!"

Of course the owner is proud because he's probably done an amazing job considering it's the first time he's done it. But, that isn't going to help him when he goes to rent or sell the home.

He wants top dollar for the home but the prospective buyers says, "Uh-uh, I ain't paying for that disaster job! I'm gonna be stuck re-doing it. I want a discount."

So, either get the expertise or hire it. It'll save you time and money in the long run.

If you don't get or hire the expertise required, you may end up regretting this mistake in judgment for many years.

That's what happened to my Dad.

WORKING MY "BUT" OFF!

I remember visiting home years later. Dad and I walked into the garage and I noticed his eyes turn downward. Silently, I started yelling at him, "Don't look! Don't look!" But my silent screams went unnoticed as his eyes landed upon the wrinkled, uneven, bumpy, many years hardened concrete.

Then came the muffled rant under his breath, "God $$*& floor looks like crap!"

Here we were some ten plus years down the track and the floor still bothered him. I thought to myself, "He saved fifty bucks or so by not hiring a concrete floor expert – was it worth it?"

Putting in the concrete floor and then my Dad's reaction years later were important lessons for me. Hopefully, I've learned from this experience. I figure, "Why skimp on skilled labor to save a couple of bucks and then regret it for years to come?"

Ten years from now are you going to miss the extra $100 you spend today to get the job done right, to get a result you're proud of years later?

Maybe I've gone too far the other way. I hire almost everything out to skilled, experienced workers. In most instances it's worked out well.

There have been a few occasions where I thought I was hiring experts and they weren't. That's a definite and very real "gotcha."

But, even in these cases, I eventually found experts and they fixed the problems. I believe this is still a better all-around result than calling my buddies over for a "fix it" party then buying pizza afterward. That's fine if you're moving a wardrobe but is that how you want to make plumbing and/or electrical repairs?

Because of the "garage floor" lesson, I spend little time working repairs. I place my focus on what needs to be done and then hire qualified, experienced experts to carry it out.

Letting experts do the work generally frees me up to go after new deals, frees me up to do more of what I really enjoy – looking for and acquiring investment property.

13 BUT, WHAT IF I LOSE MY JOB?

I worked this BUT off by jumping in the deep end. No theories. No wondering. No conjecture.

How?

Easy - I lost my job.

Mr. Vulnerable

I was in a precarious situation. I was like the guitar player in the Lawrence Welk Orchestra, the first guy to go. The orchestra can get along fine without the guitar player, nice extra but not needed!

You see, I was hired by the Wright Laboratory Advanced Propulsion Division to perform missile external aerodynamic analysis, the same group I worked for when I was in the Air Force. Then when I left the service, they hired me back.

I was very proud to get this job because it meant they were happy with the work I was doing and wanted me to continue. They were especially happy because I was doing work no one else wanted to do. In our division propulsion was the specialty not external airframe aerodynamics. But, they wanted the capability to run computer simulations on complete missile systems. In order to do that, you need to know things like ... the overall missile lift and drag.

So, the propulsion lab had two choices. First, they could figure out these numbers themselves. Or second, they could ask the flight dynamics division to tell them the answer. The flight dynamics guys are the aero experts!

Both of these options were fraught with problems. First, none of the guys in the propulsion lab wanted to do it. Finally, one guy stepped up to the plate and reluctantly took on the task. According to my co-workers, this poor fellow lasted two months and then transferred to admin work!

Next, asking the flight dynamics lab for assistance was a dead end. Somehow the answer was always "NO!" "Too busy; our projects take priority; no time" were some of the more popular excuses. But they were quick to criticize the propulsion division missile trajectory analysis for using bogus external airframe aerodynamic inputs. The flight dynamics lab would only accept numbers obtained from an industry standard aerodynamic computer program built by McDonald Douglas for NASA.

Yet, they weren't willing to help.

So, naturally, I took on the project.

Here's why.

WORKING MY "BUT" OFF!

I was the new guy. I didn't know anything about propulsion. Yet, I was working around guys who were propulsion experts. I could barely follow their conversations as they rattled off tech terms and acronyms that left me baffled. So, when I was offered the task of bringing a new capability – external airframe aerodynamic analysis – to the division, I was interested – very interested.

This could be my ticket to making a positive impact, a positive contribution; my ticket to becoming somewhat of an expert in a particular specialty.

I took on a project no one else wanted.

When I made the decision to leave the Air Force a year and a half later, my strategy paid off. The propulsion division liked my work. They wanted me to continue. They offered me a job.

Yes, bringing a new capability to the propulsion lab was great but it came with a built in problem. I was extra. I was a "nice-to-have" but not a necessity. I was doing work that could be done by the "experts" in the flight dynamics lab. I was an add-on.

As such, I was vulnerable, vulnerable to budget cuts, vulnerable to getting laid off.

I was hired in early 1993 under a twelve month contract. When the contract came up for renewal, I received a nice raise but the duration was limited to only ten months.

Why ten months?

Because in ten months the money stopped, no more funding, the program had been cancelled.

As such, in ten months, I no longer had a job. I was given plenty of notice, I knew it was coming; I appreciated the extended "heads-up."

And, why did the project get cancelled?

The political, red-tape loving, bureaucrats in Washington made a decision.

Here's what happened ...

I was supporting the Variable Flow Ducted Rocket (VFDR) program, essentially an upgrade to the Advanced Medium Range Air to Air Missile (AMRAAM). The AMRAAM is used by fighter aircraft to shoot down enemy fighter aircraft. We were looking at strapping ramjet engines to the AMRAAM and therefore effecting extending the "kill radius" by an order of magnitude. In other words, the enemy jet fighter, can't escape!

Well, it turns out our program was a threat - not to enemy fighters but to another Air Force program!

The big daddy program in the Air Force at the time was the F-22 fighter aircraft. Seemed money and materiel flowed to this program like water flowed from the Amazon to the sea.

Apparently it only took one question to cancel our program. The question went something like this, "So, Mr. Senator, if we have this new standoff air-to-air missile system then why do we need the F-22 fighter aircraft?

Shortly after this question was asked, our VFDR program was cancelled!

Unfortunately, that's how it works in Washington - money talks! Our program was cheap, low cost, affected hardly anybody, therefore it had no voice. It was speechless, dumb.

But, the F-22 ... it was BIG – REAL BIG! Contracts scattered all over the country, employing people in many states, building engines, building airframes, money flowing. Cut that program and thousands of jobs are affected, hundreds of companies affected. Many nation-wide voting districts ready to revolt! The F-22 spoke and spoke with a loud, commanding, authoritative voice!

No way was the F-22 going to be threatened by some rinky-dink missile upgrade program! Won't have it! Won't stand for it!

Logical Washington Conclusion: Cut, the cost effective rinky-dink missile upgrade program!

Ten months later, I was out of a job.

Not excited about losing my job!

I wasn't excited.

Why?

Dave Ives

First of all, I missed the pay check.

The pay check was nice. But, I learned a hard lesson when I left the Air Force - my pay dropped. It dropped by about $10,000 a year! I was doing the same job I had in the Air Force, but now – as a civilian contractor - I was doing it for less money. Not a good financial move.

Especially frustrating since I was told over and over again how military pay was not keeping up with the civilian sector. This is a classic case where theory gets crushed by reality, a lie gets exposed; truth hurts. It turns out my military pay and benefits were quite good after all.

Fortunately my Air Force exit bonus made up this $10,000 shortfall.

Well, now my pay was about to drop even more significantly as I entered the unemployment line.

The next thing I missed about my job was the work! I enjoyed what I did. It challenged my skills as an aeronautical engineer. I would often walk over to the technical library searching for appropriate books, periodicals and other research documents in order to get more insights about how to crack specific project related engineering problems.

And, we were located close to another resource rich environment – The Air Force Museum! I remember walking over to the museum to have a look at the AMRAAM. Yes, the museum had a real AMRAAM on display! I wanted to see what the mounting hooks

WORKING MY "BUT" OFF!

looked like. I was assigned to figure out the drag component for these nasty looking – but necessary – accessories.

I remember a special feeling of accomplishment when I completed a high profile assignment.

"Hey, Dave, we talked to the guys at Hughes and they say it'll cost a million bucks to run wind tunnel tests on the new missile configuration. We made a couple of changes and we want to see how it affects the overall drag. We're wondering if you could take a look at it and come up with some good numbers?" The government engineer explained.

I set about the task. I built a computer model of the new configuration and then used the industry standard MacDonald Douglas / NASA computer program to make a series of runs to determine new drag numbers. I also backed up my analysis with supporting research from a few of my technical library resources. A week later I handed in my formal cover bound report, complete with a five page write up and all the associated technical plots and graphs to support my conclusion. My analysis showed the overall missile drag would rise by 10% due to the configuration changes.

The laboratory engineering team tucked my report in a briefcase and flew off to Tucson, Arizona to meet with the Hughes engineers.

I was nervous. All those experts in Tucson would be looking at my report. My report represented the laboratory's "answer" to the question. It would be compared, measured and debated against whatever the Hughes guys came up with.

Dave Ives

When our team arrived back at Wright-Patterson, they were full of praises, "Great job Dave! The guys at Hughes were very impressed with your analysis. They all concurred with your results. You saved us a million bucks!"

Along with a great sense of relief, I also felt very proud. It was a good moment.

But, the moment wouldn't last ... the program funds were cut and I was out of a job.

And, that's why a job is financially and otherwise dangerous ... when I lost my job, two things happened:

I lost a massive chunk of my income!

I lost my role as the laboratory aero-analysis go-to guy!

Wow! That's a lot. That's a lot to lose.

And, I would suggest that for most people – especially those who enjoy what they do and have been doing it for many years - #2 above is the more damaging thing to lose! The role you play, the expertise you've accumulated, the friends you've made, the feeling of being needed, are the hardest things to let go. They're the things you miss the most. The very things that tend to keep you healthy, happy and alive!

And, did you notice that none of these things ... are things! You can't touch them. Have you ever tried to go to the store and buy a pound of experience, a loaf of "being needed," a six pack of friendship?

And, losing these things – that aren't things – is what makes losing your job so devastating. Losing the income just adds insult to injury!

For many people, losing their job is just too traumatic, too upsetting, too devastating.

I've seen the effects first hand when my Dad lost his job. You can read about it in the previous chapter, "But, what if I've got a good job?"

And, that's why I suggest, you never want to get too dependent on a job!

Here's a crazy thought … if you enjoy doing a certain line of work – JUST DO IT! Why do you have to wait for a job to come along – JUST DO IT!

In other words, if I enjoy doing aero-analysis so much, then what's stopping me?

Is there a law that says, "In order to perform aero-analysis duties you must be employed and have a job?"

NO! There isn't. I checked. It's not on the books!

Handling the job loss ...

So, I lost my job. Now what?

This is the real test ... how did I handle it.

I feel I handled it pretty well. You see, I had my Dad's experience – when he lost his job many years before - to learn from. I saw how he reacted. I chose to react differently.

Now, in fairness, my Dad had my mother and six children to support. I only had two, my wife Marieta and my daughter Franchesca. So, maybe my reaction would have been different – more like my Dad's – if I had more children. But, my main focus was on keeping a good attitude. And, I figured I had complete control – 100% - in this area. So, no matter what the situation, I could decide my attitude. I made a decision to take on each day – each challenge – with a positive attitude.

Yes, I liked my job – I liked the pay – but I wasn't overly fussed about getting laid off. I just looked at it as something that happens, you deal with it, you move on.

Financial ducks in a row

A large part of the reason for my rather carefree attitude was our financial setup. We were prepared. We were ready. We had our financial "ducks in a row."

Our financial setup was such that I didn't have to scramble for another job. My unemployment benefits would cover all our living expenses – mortgage, utilities, food and other costs.

Did we live in a shack? Did we cut back our food budget to pay for utilities? Did we make big financial sacrifices to get by?

WORKING MY "BUT" OFF!

No. No. No.

A big reason for this is we already had the habit of living below our means. We didn't spend everything and then load up the credit cards. We didn't have any credit card debt. We had one car and it was paid for, no car payments.

So, when unemployment hit, I was pleasantly surprised to discover our finances were solid. We could make it. We could hunker down for an extended period before hitting a financial wall.

A primary reason for this was the generous unemployment benefit. I received the maximum amount for a family of three. I think it was something like $900 a month. That was more than I needed to pay our living expenses. Our mortgage payment was only about $500 a month, another $50 or so for utilities, leaving $350 for food and extras.

We had a nice three bedroom home up in Huber Heights, Ohio, just outside of Dayton – no shack, good living. We had purchased the home earlier that year (1994). We got a great deal. You can read about that story in the previous chapter, "But, how do I know if it's a good buy?"

Also, I left the Air Force under a bonus program. I received an annual $10,000 payout, ongoing for twenty two years. Every December the government dropped $10,000 into my bank account! When they offered the deal, I jumped at it like a kangaroo going after a set of oncoming headlights. The Air Force wanted to reduce numbers, I was glad to volunteer.

And, I had one more source of income. Earlier that year, I invested $10,000 in a start-up computer store that was paying me a percentage of the turnover. This little side venture was bringing in an extra $100 or so a month, making the transition period between jobs a lot less stressful financially.

I met Tom at the local indoor flea market. He was selling computers and accessories. "I'm looking for investors to help me open up a computer store. I want to move out of this flea market. Would you be interested?" He proposed.

A short while later, Tom and I were knocking down walls and pulling up carpet in a rustic and dated building on Brandt Pike in Huber Heights. The new store – Disk-Go-Tech - was open within a week.

I also helped Tom drum up customers by going around to local businesses. I had an incentive; I was paid a percentage of the turnover. If I could increase the turnover, my pay went up. I remember driving all over Huber Heights talking to local business owners about their computer needs, how can Disk-Go-Tech help you solve them?

The store was a great distraction from my unemployment situation. I have fond memories of driving to the store, walking over to the nearby McDonalds and getting two large coffees – one for me and one for Tom. I enjoyed those coffee conversations hanging out at the computer store.

What about our rental property in Florida? Yes, we had it, but it wasn't making any money, probably costing us a little cash each month. So, unfortunately, our rental property in Florida was not a source of income – yet.

Going away party ... awkward

My work held a going away party for me. Well, it was really for a co-worker who landed a prestigious administration position with a hospital downtown. They added me on.

After all, how awkward would it be to have a party for a guy headed for the unemployment line? So, to make it less awkward, they included me as part of the other guy's party.

Personally, I thought it was a nice gesture and I appreciated it.

It was still awkward.

The other guy had a follow-on job. He got a slew of congratulations, pats on the back and several "Let me buy you a drink!" offers.

The reaction I received was slightly different. I was getting laid off. I didn't have a follow on job. I was headed for the unemployment line. How do you celebrate that? How do co-workers respond to that situation?

Well, I was about to find out.

Even though they had different ways of responding, my co-workers generally conveyed the same meaning, sentiment and theme. In a roundabout way they were asking, "What are you going to do? How are you going to handle being laid off? How are you going to survive without a pay check? How are you going to make it on a measly unemployment benefit?"

The party was a showcase in contrast. People congratulating my co-worker on his good fortune; landing a better job, better pay; better benefits. And then, these same people, avoiding me because they don't know what to say!

A few unfortunate souls managed to bump into me and uncomfortably took their best shot at polite dialog, "Have you got anything lined up?" or "Sorry to hear what happened?"

One female co-worker came up with probably the most honest and forthright question – a question that acknowledged the "white elephant" in the room – "Dave, are you going to be ok?"

I told you it was awkward!

Surprise, surprise!

We were not without surprises ... right after I got laid off, we found out some amazing news!

I took Marieta to the doctor because she wasn't feeling well. At this time we had no health insurance. No job therefore no insurance. Didn't matter, we went to the doc.

The doctor called me into the office. I sat down in the empty chair next to Marieta positioned in front of his big desk.

WORKING MY "BUT" OFF!

He explained, "Mr. Ives I have some good news and some bad news. First, Marieta is pregnant. It looks like twins. But, the bad news is ... they're not alive. We've got to get her up to the hospital now to have them removed."

I sat there stunned. My heart dropped to my feet. I was irritated, upset and angry at the way the doctor delivered the news. I put on a brave face.

Marieta and I walked over to the hospital located right behind the doctor's office.

As I was stood watching a flurry of activity and wondering how Marieta was doing, a nurse approached saying, "We're going to stop the procedure! We checked, there's a heartbeat, the baby is alive!"

My heart jumped up from the floor and back into my chest! I was ecstatic. It was as if our child had come back to life!

I asked about the twin. The nurse looked at me strange, "There's only one child and the child is fine."

Yes – amazing, happy, exciting news! Marieta and I were so thankful, so happy, so relieved. Our second child was on the way.

Nine months later, in late May 1995, Maria Clara was born.

Does the word 'adventure' mean anything to you?

A second child, right in the middle of a job layoff ... nice work Dave!

But, it's all part of the adventure.

That's a handy word to keep in your back pocket – adventure. It changes everything. If you think of any challenges in life as "adventure", you can deal with it better. At least that's my experience. If something comes along that looks daunting, tough, ugly, nasty, I just label it "adventure." I can hardly wait to see how I deal with it! Imagine the stories I can tell when it's all over?

Medical insurance anyone?

One of the first tasks I undertook following the discovery that we had a child on the way is to look for medical insurance.

I called a number of insurers and arrived at the same result, NO DEAL. Not one would cover us for pregnancy. Marieta was already pregnant – they wouldn't touch it.

I could get medical insurance for other ailments but the cost-benefit was ridiculous. The basic plan included a $10,000 deductible then they start paying 80% of the bills. All for the low, low price of $400 a month or more!

I quickly determined we would go without insurance. I would pay our medical costs out of pocket, out of our savings, out of our highly scaled back income.

But, it turns out I didn't have to.

I discovered something amazing about the United States, about the state of Ohio. While standing in line to pay my first medical bill, I remember turning the bill over and reading some big bold print as follows:

If you make below (I forget the dollar amount), ***you do not have to pay this bill.***

My unemployment benefits were good, but not that good. When I got to the booth and informed the lady I was unemployed and receiving benefits, she stamped the bill paid.

I was stunned. I was fully prepared to pay. I had no idea there was such a system in place, a safety net for low income folks.

From that point forward we were placed on a program for expectant parents and we didn't have to pay for any of it. I was pleasantly surprised.

And, to top it off, Marieta and I both agreed the care and facilities were top quality, much better than our experience at Wright-Patterson hospital where our first daughter was born.

Under the free government program, Marieta had regular appointments downtown with quality doctors and nurses. Some care involved going to the hospital – the Miami Valley Hospital in downtown Dayton. Top quality facility, top quality staff and top quality care. Our daughter was born in this hospital. The staff appeared much more experienced and professional than those at the military hospital.

In other words, the free government service was better than my job benefit service. I found this a bit disturbing. Why would the quality of service go up when I wasn't paying for it? Why was the quality of service lower when I was an active duty military member working for the benefit?

I never would have thought that losing my job would allow me to get such quality medical service for my family. Nor did I ever think it would come at a lower cost, no cost, free.

I wasn't thrilled about having others – taxpayers – pay for my medical care, but I figured it was only temporary and we wouldn't abuse the system. But, prior to this, I didn't even know the system existed. I stumbled onto it.

Getting tested

Now, I was fully entrenched with my jobless situation. I was in it. I had to deal with it.

This is the test. How do you deal with adversity? As they say, it's not so much what happens to you in life - it's how you handle it, how you deal with it?

Well, I was getting tested.

WORKING MY "BUT" OFF!

A phrase from my military days applied. A phrase my commander used to use whenever he handed me a particularly nasty assignment, "Dave, this is your opportunity to excel!"

First, I made up my mind to stay positive. Keep my attitude positive, uplifted, goal oriented. After all, it's probably easier to get a new job if I convey confidence as opposed to conveying doom and gloom!

I felt confident in my skills and confident in my ability to secure another job.

I would get up every day, jump out of bed, go for a jog and then get dressed as if I was going to my previous job. My attire included a sport coat and tie. I would then go looking for a job.

I also had side excursions to the unemployment office and medical appointments with Marieta.

The unemployment line

I used to get some looks while waiting in the unemployment line wearing my sport coat and tie. I was virtually the only one dressed up. Even the folks working behind the counter looked run down. It was not the place to be if you were looking for a confidence boost, self-esteem uplift. Folks gave me a common look that spoke to me, "What are you doing here? If you can afford clothes like that, then you don't need unemployment benefits."

I didn't mind too much. I figured I was standing there for my family. I would take a bit of embarrassment to feed my family.

And, I also felt it was a temporary situation. I wasn't going to be coming down here for very long.

The doctor's office

Marieta didn't have a driver's license yet so I was the chauffeur. I attended all her medical appointments.

Sitting in the waiting room with my fancy shoes, sport coat and tie, I'd get some cross-eyed looks. The other ladies in the room – I don't remember ever seeing any men - would stare at me wondering ... "What's he doing here?"

After all, this was medical care for low income folks. I got their drift – I didn't look low income. And yet, I was – but only temporarily, at that moment.

I was working hard to change my situation.

And, that's where I was different. I was hustling to get out of this temporary low income situation. And yes, we were low income, but we weren't broke. I got the feeling that wasn't the case for the others. They gave off the impression that low income was a way of life, both in the past and for the future as well. I could be wrong – and I hope I'm wrong - but that's the feeling I had when observing and listening to the others during my weekly trips to the medical appointment waiting room.

Job hunting

I remember sending off tons of resumes. And, I remember getting back lots of rejection letters. I didn't worry too much because I felt it was all part of the process. I figured it would take a lot of hunting to find a job. I figured it would take work. I was prepared to do the work.

I applied to a local aircraft propeller manufacturing company. I remember the nice rejection letter they sent. It implied they had an overwhelming pool of qualified applicants for the position. There was some serious competition for engineering jobs. Lots of skilled applicants, few positions available!

I applied for jobs directly with the government. I was targeting jobs at Wright-Patterson in the labs or on the other side of the base with the Foreign Technology Division. But, word came out the government had a hiring freeze in place. Landing a government job was pretty much off the table.

Breaking the news to mom and dad

How I handled my job loss is probably best exemplified in a phone conversation with my parents.

A couple of weeks into my unemployed status the phone rang, it was Mom ...

"Oh, yeah Mom, we're all fine. Doin great." I stated with a spring in my voice.

"And how are you and Dad? Enjoying life with all the kids gone?" I quickly smacked the conversation tennis ball back into her court.

Mom responded by the book, "We're fine too. Nothing much new here."

Then a pause and finally out came the question, the real question, the real reason for the phone call, "Oh yeah - by the way Dave - how's everything with your job?"

I told her months ago my position was going away. I told her the story, how the government program I was working on was losing its funding.

I'd been expecting the question and I was ready with the answer. Well, it wasn't really an answer, but my response pretty much summed up my attitude, when I replied sharply, "What job?"

"What do you mean, What Job, David?" she replied in a Don't-Joke-With-Me fashion.

"Mom, remember I told you a while back my job was going away, they're cutting the program? Well it went away about two weeks ago. I don't have a job."

The next sound I heard was a "thud" – the sound of the phone crashing against the wall as it dangled by the chord. Before it crashed a second time, I heard my Dad's voice, "What's this about you not having a job?"

WORKING MY "BUT" OFF!

"Dad, it's no big deal. They ran out of funding and I'm out of work. I'm not the first guy to get laid off from a job."

"How come you didn't tell me?" he growled.

"Dad, why would I want to tell you I lost my job? That's not exciting news. And, besides, I told you a while ago they were cutting the program and my job was going away. We're fine Dad. Don't worry."

I tried to convince him it's no big deal.

My Dad switched gears from dismay and distress to care and concern, "You need some money?"

I have to admit, I really liked hearing him say that. We didn't need any money, but what a feeling to know my Dad was right there if we did. That's powerful stuff to know your Mom and Dad are there for you. I never wanted to take that for granted so I would only accept money if absolutely necessary. But, man is it great to know you've got family ready to help.

"Dad, we're fine. If I needed money you'd be the first one I'd call." I said in a confident tone.

And I meant it. I wouldn't hesitate to ask my Dad for money – if I needed it. But, I didn't and it would be irresponsible for me to accept money – or ask for money - when I didn't need it.

After that exchange I could feel my Dad's mood change. His mood changed from "What's wrong with you son?" to "My son is handling it. He's ok. He's got it. I'm proud of him."

Although, my Dad could not understand or relate to my calmness about getting laid off, he seemed to believe I had it under control. And, I did.

This simple interchange with my father was a crowning moment in my financial life. I was changing. I was growing. I was developing the correct attitude and mindset for breaking the chains of my JOB (just over broke) condition.

Happy ending

About one month into my unemployment, I received a phone call, "Dave, we'll be sending out an offer package. We're hoping you accept it." The representative from Ball Aerospace Corporation delivered the good news.

I landed a position supporting the Flight Dynamics Lab as a contractor. I'd have an office on base at the lab and one at the company building in Fairborn, Ohio located right across the street from Wright State University. My short lived unemployment "adventure" was over.

I called Dad and told him the news.

He was very happy.

14 BUT, WHERE DO I GO FROM HERE?

I've finally figured out I'll probably never finish working my BUT off!

And that's because ... the BUT questions keep coming!

I suppose that's a good thing. As long as I don't let them get the better of me and I just keep working them off, I should be OK.

And, here's another thought provoking BUT question –

BUT, where do I go from here?

I like this question because it's a lifesaver! It's the question that keeps me going. It's the one that keeps me focused and on track.

How?

Well, I can use it for virtually any situation – positive or negative, good or bad. Then I can focus on the result I want. I can choose my attitude. I can determine my next step, my course correction, my next adventure.

I can almost hear you asking, "What is he talking about?"

So, here's where I put on my thinking cap, searching for the best way to explain myself ... I can hardly wait to read what I come up with!

Here goes nothing!

When life's good ...

For instance, let's say you just reached a big goal, a dream you've had for many years is now a reality.

Say, you've just achieved financial independence and you've left the JOB world. You're happy. You're excited. You're relieved. You're proud. Life's good!

And now for the question that puts it all in perspective, the question that brings you back to earth. Just two words, but they're powerful - "Now what?"

Put another way, "Where do I go from here?"

So, you've "made it", what are you going to do for an encore? Are you just going to sit around all day patting yourself on the back? Wouldn't that get a bit old after a while – after a very short while?

If you don't set the next goal – the next milestone – you're setting yourself up for danger. You've reached a plateau and it's nice but who wants to sit there for very long? Especially, when you look up and see the next mountain peak and wonder, "Can I climb that high?"

You may find yourself longing for the "struggle" days, longing for the days when you were "hungry!"

Strange as it may seem, life has a tendency to bury the "good ole days" in the struggle! The struggle seems to be the "flavor" of life, it's where the best tasting bits are located, it's where the great stories are found, it's where you discover what you're made of; who you really are.

So, where do I go from here?

Now, it's time to set the next goal, the next adventure; the next dream. It's time to set out on another journey.

When life's not so good ...

What about when life appears to throw you a monkey wrench, when things aren't going so well, when disaster strikes?

Doesn't the same question apply?

Isn't it appropriate to ask, "Now what?"

"Where do I go from here?"

When disaster strikes me – it has and will again – I need to remember something very powerful - I am in complete control ... of my thoughts! I'm in complete control of how I choose to view the situation. I'm in complete control of my attitude. I need to take responsibility for my behavior – my response!

For instance, if I've crashed and burned – failed – in a business project, how do I respond?

OK, I've failed – now what?

Do I start crying? Do I blame it on everyone else but me?

Or, do I gather myself together and pose the question, "Where do I go from here?"

By the way, I've been there! I've been through a business disaster, lost buckets of money. The cash flew away from me like a hurricane on its way out of town, leaving my finances in a state of devastation and destruction!

The question, "But, where do I go from here?" saved me. It didn't save me from losing lots of money, but it saved me from crying about it, it saved me from blaming others, it saved me from inaction.

I kept my wits about me. I got up dusted myself off and proceeded to conduct property deals essentially gaining back all the money I'd lost. It took me about three years to finally pull off this turnaround, but I did it. And, I did it by focusing on the important question, "Where do I go from here?" instead of the useless question "How could I be so stupid to invest in that business?"

WORKING MY "BUT" OFF!

I kind of looked at the situation this way. Let's say we decided to climb Mt. Everest and half way up we discover something's wrong – very wrong.

We forgot to bring the warm jackets.

Now what?

Is it going to do us any good to complain, to place blame, to argue about who's at fault?

Not really. How's any of that going to keep us warm? It won't.

We're in the situation now. Doesn't really matter how we got here, the reality is – we are ... we must deal with it or die.

So, we can point fingers, yell at each other, scream and complain or we can ask, "Where do we go from here?"

"Now what?"

"What's next?"

Get our attitudes in check and move quickly down off the mountain and save our lives!

We may end up missing a nose, a few fingers and toes, but we're alive, we made it. It beats the heck out of being dead!

And that's how I view my business disaster. I lost a lot of financial flesh, but luckily my financial nose, fingers and toes grew back!

Thank God, I resisted the temptation to feel sorry for myself, to blame others, to sit in the corner sucking my thumb and sulking! Don't think I didn't want to!

It appears that no matter what happens to me or you in life – either good or bad - we're always going to be faced with this question, "NOW WHAT?"

So, I like to throw out a few questions for you to ponder. Some questions to get your creative juices flowing, to get you in the mood for action, to get you ready to jump on your next adventure!

> *Ok, you've got a crappy job, pay is bad, work is boring; hours are terrible; you don't like it - now what? What are you planning to do about it?*
>
> *Ok, you've just been laid off from your dream job – interesting assignments, high pay, great benefits, and great work environment - now what? What's your plan of attack?*
>
> *Ok, you've just sold your massively successful business for millions – now what? What challenging project have you got lined up next?*
>
> *Ok, you've built a very profitable property portfolio and now you're a full time property investor. You're pumped, you're excited - you've done it! Now what? What are you going to do for an encore?*

Ok, you've got millions from your last successful business venture. In the last six months you've done ... EVERYTHING – all the dreams you've been putting off for years! Then you wake up one morning with a horrifying realization - you're bored out of your mind! Now what? What are you going to do to keep the creative juices flowing?

This book is my "Now what?" project. In July 2009 I quit my JOB and haven't looked back. I reached my goal – financial independence.

So, I asked myself, "Now what?"

News flash! Hey, what if there are other folks who want to achieve financial independence? What if there are folks who want it but don't believe it's possible for them?

Why couldn't I share some of my experiences, some of my trials, some of my triumphs with others so they can see – they can believe – it's possible! Not just possible for me, but for them as well. After all, if this guy can do it – anyone can!

So, it's over to you.

Now that you've read the book ... "What's next?"

What's next for you?

Where do you go from here?

Dave Ives

Wishing you every success and all the best on your journey through the biggest adventure of all – life!

Share your insights, reflections and feedback. Write a heartfelt review on amazon.com and/or goodreads.com.

RECOMMENDED READING LIST

1. <u>Rich Dad, Poor Dad</u> by Robert Kiyosaki. Great book for developing a business-like mindset. Easy to read and understand. Once you read this book you'll be hooked and start knocking off the other books in the "Rich Dad" series.

2. <u>How to Make a Living without a Job</u> by Barbara J. Winter. A must read if you want to exit the JOB world and enter the realm of the "joyfully jobless!"

3. <u>Trump. How to Get Rich</u> by Donald J. Trump. I used to listen a lot to the mainstream media. As such I had a severe negative slant in my opinion of Mr. Trump. That all changed when I started reading his books. He's got a lot of wisdom – business and otherwise – to share. All backed up by amazing life and business success.

4. <u>Million Dollar Habits</u> by Robert J. Ringer. This book rocks! It's a no-nonsense, no-excuse, treatise on developing success habits.

5. <u>Trump Stategies for Real Estate</u> by George H. Ross. Amazing negotiation strategies! Yes, these are big dollar deals but the

principles apply for virtually all transactions both large and small.

6. <u>Think and Grow Rich</u> by Napolean Hill. This is the one of the most powerful success books ever! The wisdom is timeless. It's easy and - dare I say – fun to read. The author challenges the reader to uncover "the secret." It's in the book but not spelled out explicitly. What a great technique - keeps the reader focused, keeps the reader searching for "the secret!"

7. <u>The Wealth Power of Property</u> by Fred and Brett Johnson. Best explanation I've found for why residential property is at the top of the list when it comes to wealth vehicles!

8. <u>Building Wealth through Investment Property</u> by Jan Somers. This lady knows what she's talking about! She's a pro, a very successful property investor. And, aren't we lucky she's written this book to share her extensive insights and experience!

ABOUT THE AUTHOR

Dave Ives was born in Melrose, Massachusetts and raised in Pelham, New Hampshire. He served in the United States Air Force from 1981 until 1992, and then worked as a civilian engineer. In July 2009, he left the engineering world to focus full time on his property investing business. In 2014 Dave published his first book starting another career as an author.

Dave currently resides in Alice Springs, Northern Territory, Australia.

For more about Dave, visit his website ivesguy.com.

Other books by Dave Ives:

> Live Free or Die
> Dreams of the Philippines
> Perception is Reality
> Yanks in the Outback: *A Story of Woomera, South Australia, the Joint Defense Facility Nurrungar (JDFN) and the First Gulf War.*

www.ingramcontent.com/pod-product-compliance
Lightning Source LLC
Chambersburg PA
CBHW070854180526
45168CB00005B/1814